PRAISE FOR
THE SPIRIT-LED LEADER

"His insights forged in the fires of experience, Tim Geoffrion has written a gem of a book on leadership. He's avoided the euphemisms and lists of 'easy steps' that so often plague books on this subject and instead given us a work that will be a blessing to anyone who wants to lead in a Christ-centered manner. At turns inspirational and practical, *The Spirit-Led Leader* charts a course that is both hopeful and challenging. If Christian leaders base their work on these words, there's no telling the kingdom work that can happen!"

TONY JONES, national coordinator of Emergent Village

"I had to smile when I read Timothy Geoffrion's description of himself: 'trying harder, being nicer, being less nice, reading more books...hiring better people, firing the wrong people, being more assertive, being less assertive, and even praying more,' but still feeling frustrated and disappointed as a leader. It is so *real!* Geoffrion's book offers us a foundation for leadership beyond human striving. He points us instead to profound dependence upon the grace of God at work in us. Read this book, engage the practices, and be guided into a deeper connection between your soul and your leadership."

RUTH HALEY BARTON, author of *Invitation to Solitude and Silence*

"Timothy Geoffrion has given us much practical, helpful advice for ways to turn to God in our personal lives and organizational leadership, drawing steadily on biblical wisdom and confirmation as well as on his own and others' extensive experience."

TILDEN EDWARDS, founder and
senior fellow of the Shalem Institute for Spiritual Formation

"Tim has written a fine book. It comes out of his experience as a pastor, CEO, and human being. He is a superb teacher. But best of all, he lives what he teaches. The material in the book is like the substance of his life, which I have known for the past five years."

JOHN ACKERMAN, author of *Listening to God*

"Tim Geoffrion's book provides practical tools for strengthening a leader's service in any complex organization. Reflecting on his personal experience through the lenses of his faith and values, he identifies what has worked and what has not worked quite as well in the places he has served. Geoffrion's book helps leaders develop and apply attitudes and skills appropriate to their setting."

CHERYL F. DUDLEY, associate executive director
of the National Ministries of American Baptist Churches USA

The Spirit-Led Leader

The
Spirit-Led
Leader

Nine Leadership Practices and Soul Principles

Timothy C. Geoffrion

THE
ALBAN
INSTITUTE
Herndon, Virginia
www.alban.org

The Alban Institute
2121 Cooperative Way, Suite 100
Herndon, VA 20171-3025

Scripture quotations marked NRSV are from the New Revised Standard Version of the Bible, copyright © 1989, Division of Christian Education of the National Council of Churches of Christ in the United States of America, and are used by permission.

Scripture quotations marked NIV are from the Holy Bible, New International Version, copyright © 1973, 1978, 1984, International Bible Society, and are used by permission of Zondervan Publishing House.

Cover design by Adele Robey, Phoenix Graphics.

Library of Congress Cataloging-in-Publication Data

Geoffrion, Timothy C., 1957-
  The spirit-led leader : nine leadership practices and soul
principles / Timothy C. Geoffrion ; foreword by Thomas Gillespie.
    p. cm.
  Includes bibliographical references.
  ISBN-13: 978-1-56699-317-3
  ISBN-10: 1-56699-317-2
  1. Christian leadership. 2. Christian leadership—Biblical
teaching. 3. Clergy—Religious life. I. Title.

  BV652.1.G44 2005
  253—dc22
                              2005026480

        09 08 07 06 05   UG   1 2 3 4 5

My prayer is that God will speak through this book to encourage and help Christian pastors, executives, staff members, and lay leaders to deepen their love for God and to serve more effectively as spiritual leaders, as they seek to fulfill the mission and objectives of their organization.

CONTENTS

Chapter 1   The Vision
Leadership Practice   Envision your leadership flowing
out of a deep spiritual life.
Soul Principle   Fruitfulness in leadership requires
the work of God in and through us.

Chapter 2   Connecting to God
Leadership Practice   Actively cultivate your own
spiritual life.
Soul Principle   Spiritual vitality flows from a
real change of heart and mind
toward God.

FOREWORD

A neglected gift to the Church by the Protestant Reformers was the recovery of a biblical understanding of vocation, the conviction that believers are called to a specific task in the world that is informed and empowered by Christian faith. Luther could claim with a straight face that the scullery maid on her knees scrubbing the kitchen floor renders more effective service to God than the priest on his knees at prayer in the chapel. John Calvin, who taught that the work-a-day world is "the arena for the glorification of God," was allegedly asked by a skeptic if that meant Christian cobblers made Christian shoes. "No," replied Calvin, "it means they make good shoes." Few Christians of Protestant persuasion today would readily understand or agree with either Reformer.

In *The Spirit-Led Leader,* Timothy Geoffrion recaptures this important insight and makes it accessible to a postmodern generation by reacting to it in terms of institutional *leadership* and Christian *spirituality*. Writing out of his pastoral and managerial experience in the church and para-church organizations, the executive director and president of Family Hope Services makes a compelling case for authentically blending administrative and spiritual leadership. Although designed for pastors, executives, administrators, managers, and coordinators who wish to fulfill their "God-given purpose" in Christian organizations, this book also provides guidance for those who seek to serve God vocationally in secular settings.

While American popular culture today tends to divorce spirituality from religion (as in the common disclaimer, "I am very spiritual but not at all religious"), Geoffrion defines the term in a Christian context simply and straightforwardly as "our sense of connection to God"—namely, the One who is Other than a dimension of the human ego or of the created universe. The reality of this relationship, based as it is according to the New Testament upon grace as God's unmerited, undeserved, and unearned love, impacts a believer's life in a manner analogous to the way in which we are influenced by those significant others in our lives who love us and whom we love. Our author devoted much of his book to pointing up the ways (disciplines) in which our relationship to God can be strengthened, developed, enriched, and even shared. For it is his deep conviction that the God and Father of our Lord Jesus Christ is One who actually works in human life in transforming, illuminating, and empowering ways. In this regard, the reader is encouraged to move quickly to chapter eight where Geoffrion offers personal and moving testimony to our human struggle to trust God with our lives.

Spirituality, thus understood, is crucial for organizational leadership because there is more to administrative and managerial responsibilities than establishing goals and meeting deadlines. Other dimensions underscored here are the emotional, relational, psychological, and spiritual aspects of working together with others. Leading a team, a staff, a department, or an institution requires "multi-dimensional, holistic" skills. It is important to note that our author is not talking about how to be pious (spiritual) or even pastoral on the job. His point is that our relationship with God informs and empowers the task we are given. Leadership entails sharing that vision of and enthusiasm for the common endeavor with those who are colleagues. Thus Geoffrion contends that "every aspect of leadership is influenced by our spirituality," meaning by that simply, "our sense of connection to God."

Individual chapters develop this theme by treating such crucial issues as envisioning leadership flowing out of a deep spiritual life, activity cultivating one's spiritual life, developing specific spiritual disciplines, seeking to serve God's purposes, creating a vital spiritual environment within the workplace, making change a personal priority, leading by listening, trusting God, and opening oneself fully to the love and grace of God. Each topic is developed with ample attention to analysis and theory, and each concludes with a practice section under such rubrics as "Questions for Reflection," "Instructions for Triads" (discussion groups), or "Something to Think About."

This is not another "self-help" book. As the title intimates, leadership is fundamentally a matter of being led by Another. "To align our will with God's will means that we believe and behave as if God is our personal leader and the leader of our ministry or organization," Geoffrion contends. In a word, *The Spirit-Led Leader* is a worthy resource for all, whether scullery maid or cobbler or executive director, who desire to *connect* with God by faith not only personally but vocationally as well.

Thomas W. Gillespie
President Emeritus
Princeton Theological Seminary

PREFACE

This book is about effective spiritual leadership. I want to encourage and equip men and women to become powerful spiritual leaders, people whose spiritual life is central to their personal identity and approach to leadership. I have a heart for those who want to make a positive impact in their workplace but struggle to produce the results they envision—for their organization, for their co-workers or staff, or for themselves. I write also for those who are not designated leaders or chairpersons of leadership teams, but who want to contribute to the leadership of their organization, and to experience spiritually vital working relationships.

As individuals, we have much to look forward to as God continues to work in our lives. As leaders, we can also anticipate great things as God inspires and empowers our leadership. We can expect God to work in us and through us in meaningful and life-changing ways. The key to experiencing all that God has in mind for us is to know what God offers and to learn to cooperate productively with God's workings in our life and leadership.

The "abundant life" Jesus promised to those who trust in him and his leadership (John 10:10) does not reflect pie-in-the-sky optimism; it is not reserved for a select few. Life and leadership are full of struggle, disappointments, and heartaches, but we may always have hope, knowing that God works in and through those who love God and seek to serve God's purposes.

Paul described our hope for an enduring relationship with God and a meaningful life of service this way:

> For it is by grace you have been saved, through faith—and this not from yourselves, it is the gift of God—not by works, so that no one can boast. For we are God's workmanship, created in Christ Jesus to do good works, which God prepared in advance for us to do.
>
> Ephesians 2:8-10 NIV

God's gracious and active work in our lives, despite our limitations, failings, or troubles, gives us hope because our future depends more on God than on us. God's grace not only brings forgiveness but also enables us to live out our God-given purpose in life; that is, the "good works, which God prepared in advance for us to do." God's power to vitalize life and ministry is available to everyone who believes, but those who aspire to spiritual leadership need to learn key leadership practices and soul principles to become effective leaders. My goal is to help all who see themselves as leaders, both those officially appointed or elected and those who find themselves in situations where leadership is needed. I want to help leaders better experience what God has in mind for them as precious children of God, anointed to lead—both for the sake of Christ's kingdom and for the benefit of all who work together in a ministry, church, or business.

More than 20 years as an ordained minister, college and seminary teacher, and nonprofit executive have taught me important principles and practices of spirituality and leadership. I have come to see that serving as an effective spiritual leader requires a solid foundation of grace and a vital, growing spiritual life. We need to break down any false dichotomy in our thinking between leadership and spiritual life, to integrate them, and ultimately to allow our spiritual life to transform our leadership.

On the surface, providing effective organizational leadership—whether as vision caster, strategic planner, manager, supervisor, or coordinator—may appear to be quite different from offering meaningful spiritual leadership. Organizational leadership tends to focus on the organization's stated objectives and on the work of leading team members to accomplish them. Spiritual leadership cultivates a vibrant spiritual atmosphere in the workplace and among team members, including, where appropriate, such activities as incorporating biblical and theological knowledge in setting values and policy, promoting spiritual practices among workers, holding corporate worship, strengthening community life, and giving opportunities for service.

I have come to see, however, that organizational and spiritual leadership responsibilities overlap far more than I once thought. While each set of activities has its own character, every aspect of leadership is influenced by our spirituality—consciously or unconsciously. Christians who aspire to be vital and effective leaders will lead in ways that draw on their spiritual lives to the maximum degree possible.

The more I have sought to lead from a strong spiritual base, the more I have experienced a sense of integrity and coherence in my leadership, and the more powerful have been the results. Such leadership is partly an art, partly a result of careful planning, and always a working of the grace of God. Earnestly seeking God and God's working in our personal lives and in our organizations is essential to becoming effective spiritual leaders.

Most of the ideas expressed in this book have been validated through my own experience as a leader. I have wrestled with leadership issues and have sought biblical and spiritual insights to help me become more effective. I do not claim to have mastered the art of spiritual leadership. On the contrary, at times I've been a slow and awkward learner who understands these concepts better in theory than in practice. Nevertheless, I have experienced gratifying results from the effort I have put into learning new ways of leading and of drawing God more consciously into the workings of our organization. I'm eager to pass on the gleanings from my own trial-and-error attempts at personal growth and leadership.

ACKNOWLEDGMENTS

The Spirit-Led Leader came into being largely because many Spirit-led people have greatly enriched my life. At the top of the list is my wife, Jill, who has modeled seeking God in deep and transforming ways and has continually encouraged me to keep growing in my spiritual life and experience. Jill is a tremendously perceptive and insightful spiritual leader in our home and professionally, as an author and ordained minister. She has been a great source of wisdom to me over the years. She urged me to take my first weeklong spiritual retreat in 1998 in Taizé, France. Her commitment to mysticism has opened my eyes to new ways of relating to God. I would never have been able to complete the book had it not been for her ongoing encouragement and self-sacrificial support of my long hours of writing in the evenings and on the weekends.

John Ackerman, my spiritual director, has taught me many helpful spiritual practices, including regularly listening for God's voice. He consistently reminds me to bring my questions and concerns to God in prayer early in the process of problem-solving, as opposed to stewing and mentally agonizing over troubling issues. He showed me how to teach co-workers to look for God's activity in the midst of our working together—an approach that helped me to cultivate a richer spiritual environment at work.

My ability to serve effectively as a spiritual leader has also been greatly enhanced by a course of study directed by the Shalem Institute, in Bethesda, Maryland, called "The Soul of the Executive." After years of struggling with the tension I felt between serving both as a strong administrative leader and as a spiritual leader, I was introduced to helpful literature and thinking on spirituality and leadership.

A course requirement of "The Soul of the Executive" was a practical project to integrate spirituality and my executive leadership. One outcome was a series of initiatives I have led at Family Hope Services, where I serve as executive director and president. Family Hope is a Christian-based, nonprofit organization that runs TreeHouse, an outreach for at-risk youth in multiple locations in the Minneapolis suburbs. Family Hope's spiritual initiatives are called "Seeking God Together." The book studies, spiritual practices, Bible studies, and new ways of seeking corporate discernment in decision-making have not only changed me; they have transformed the way I go about serving as a spiritual leader in the workplace.

I especially want to acknowledge the supportive role that the board of directors and my co-workers at Family Hope Services have played throughout the writing of this book. Family Hope sponsored my course of study at Shalem and has generously provided time for me to participate in annual spiritual retreats, to teach workshops, and to conduct seminars on spirituality and spiritual leadership—and even to write for days at a time on occasion. I could not have produced this book without staff members' participation in "Seeking God Together" initiatives and without their ongoing support of my research and writing.

Many of the ideas expressed in this book have been sharpened and developed thanks to the honest and insightful comments made by John Hogenson, Cheryl Dudley, Jonathan Reckford, and John Ackerman, who carefully read an early version of *The Spirit-Led Leader*. I am deeply grateful for their investment into this work, as I am for my two Alban editors, Beth Gaede and Jean Caffey Lyles, whose suggestions were immensely helpful. Finally, I am deeply grateful to all of my students over the years, who have broadened and refined my thinking. They have challenged my teaching and helped me to understand better how God works in their life and leadership. Ultimately, I have written *The Spirit-Led Leader* for them.

INTRODUCTION

Leadership was much harder than I had imagined it would be and less satisfying than I had hoped, until I finally began to make some fundamental changes in how I thought about leadership and went about trying to lead.

For years, I didn't see the results I wanted and couldn't figure out why. I tried working harder, being nicer, being less nice, reading more books, attending more seminars, hiring better-qualified people, firing people who were wrong for the job, being more assertive, being less assertive, and even praying more. I tried to use all the available tools and resources, and many helped to one degree or another. Still, I often felt frustrated and disappointed.

As I worked with staff members and volunteers, I kept running into conflicts that caught me by surprise or eluded easy resolution. At times I grew weary of the emotional ups and downs and personnel issues—and it showed. I would become impatient, irritable, and annoyed when staff members' feelings repeatedly got in the way of the work to be done. I would crack the whip and try to push staff to set higher goals, work harder, and produce more measurable results. Though I tried to listen empathically, I would often cut conversations short so that we could all get back to work.

Although I might appear warm and friendly on the outside, I was often doing a slow boil inside. I wanted staff to get the job done efficiently and effectively, with a minimum of complaints and distractions. I often viewed personnel issues as annoyances and a waste of time. I allowed myself to become so task-oriented at times that it was as if I had forgotten I was working with human beings, not just ideas and machines.

In the end, my strong, results-oriented, no-nonsense leadership style proved to be not only a strength—keeping the organization focused and moving toward corporate goals—but also a weakness. My overemphasis on outcomes too often undermined my ability to create the positive, constructive, and spiritually rich environment that I hoped for.

I'm not alone, of course. Strong leaders, in general, can be results-oriented to a fault. Sometimes our driven nature and our focus on the vision, mission, strategies, and desired outcomes blinds us to what is needed to bring about success in the right kind of way. That is, we may come up with great ideas, have the best of intentions for leading, and be "wired" to lead the charge, but lack the necessary attitudes, insights, or skills to address other important dimensions of leadership: the emotional, relational, psychological, and spiritual aspects of working with others.

We may fear that if we cater to every need, desire, or concern of staff members, we will never get anywhere. We may simply feel beyond our depth in dealing with the various demands and viewpoints of our co-workers. We may feel so driven to complete tasks and to achieve that we come to view contrary views or the relational and emotional needs of others as distractions from what "really matters"—that is, our corporate goals and objectives. Rather than learn how to relate constructively to co-workers and how to create helpful processes to motivate and draw on the strengths of the entire team, we may find it easier to focus on numbers, facilities, size of operation, dollars, salary, status, prestige, and other external or self-oriented performance measures.

Sometimes our natural drive to lead with excellence leaves us frustrated, confused, angry, and discouraged, especially when our staff members don't seem to want to cooperate or "get with the program." Then, because we don't know how to inspire people and lead them effectively, we let our negative feelings spill over onto the staff, or we employ thinly veiled strategies to manipulate them to do what we want. They become upset, cynical, or simply unmotivated, and the effectiveness of our leadership deteriorates further.

Because of our painful and frustrating experiences, we may be tempted to conclude that is impossible to attend both to the needs of the organization as a whole and to those of the staff who do the work. Indeed, we may wonder, is it even possible to be *both* a strong, results-oriented leader *and* a caring, spiritual leader to the staff?

When our results-oriented paradigms and personalities drive us to overfocus on accomplishing our personal goals or corporate objectives to the point of alienating or neglecting our co-workers and staff members, something is out of whack. If we persist in this imbalance, we won't be effective leaders in the long run. Also, we will miss out on much of what we could experience as multidimensional, holistic leaders—that is, leaders who are attuned to the physical, emotional, mental, and spiritual well-being of the workers, as well as to the quality of the work they produce. The "what" and the "how" of our work must be kept in balance. How we work with others to accomplish corporate goals must be appropriately balanced with what we seek to accomplish as an organization. How staff members are treated and how they feel about working in an organization must not be minimized in the pursuit of results.

In other words, a results-oriented model of leadership is grossly deficient if it disrespects, devalues, or fails to attend to the needs of team members. Leading in this way is shortsighted and counterproductive. Furthermore, an excessively results-oriented environment may produce outcomes that are shallow at best and dangerous at worst. The results will be shallow when we neglect quality in pursuit of quantity, when we are satisfied with form over substance, or when we tout organizational success while giving short shrift to our core values. For example, if a church doubles or triples its membership or builds a beautiful facility, yet people's lives are not being transformed or staff members feel manipulated or devalued, something is missing from this picture of "success."

In time, an overemphasis on results within the corporate culture may actually be dangerous for those who work in the organization—and in the case of a church, for the people of the congregation. Any organization that places undue value on achievement, appearance, and status places increasing pressure on people to perform for one another. People who believe that others are determining their worth mainly on the basis of how well they seem to "have it together" and the results they produce may be tempted to hide their struggles and inflate their successes. Hypocritical posturing and judging of one another may increase. The environment may become psychologically and emotionally unsafe and even debilitating for those who struggle to measure up. Even those skilled enough to perform well may risk intolerable levels of stress and burnout—levels that may seriously impede their ability to be caring co-workers within the organization, and loving spouses and parents at home.[1]

Why? As limited, fallible human beings, we are dependent on the grace of God and one another for life. We function best in environments where grace is valued, care and support are offered to individuals, appropriate performance standards are maintained, and significant opportunities are given to contribute to the success of the organization.[2] High expectations bring out the best in us, inspiring us to contribute significantly as workers and community participants, but the standards should not be so high that we feel pressured to be dishonest or ruthless. Leaders who overfocus on results and performance, without an adequate measure of grace and genuine concern for the well-being of their workers, will eventually make people feel that it is unsafe to be honest, vulnerable, and open to seek or receive the kind of support they need.

Of course driven, results-oriented leaders are not the only ones who can get out of balance. For example, those on the other end of the leadership style spectrum may be consumed with pleasing or caring for co-workers—a different kind of results orientation. For those in this category, an overemphasis on "results" looks quite different. Instead of focusing on completing tasks and meeting corporate goals, we are preoccupied with personal popularity or the feelings of staff members.

Leadership that overemphasizes people is doomed to failure and disappointment. If our main goal is to be liked by everyone, we are going to fail to do something that needs to be done for the sake of the team (in an effort to avoid conflict, for example). We may fear that our action will alienate a team member, without realizing that our inaction will likely annoy or frustrate someone else. If we are truly motivated to be caring people who show God's love and grace to our co-workers, we may have the best of intentions, but we may wind up with a different kind of leadership frustration—results that fail to earn the respect and approval of our board, constituents, or donors.

Our concern for our staff members and the people of our organization has gone too far when we neglect our responsibility to keep the mission of the organization central in our thinking and leading. We get out of balance and become ineffective when we as leaders allow the priority of the team to shift from effectively serving Christ's purposes in the world, however we may define them in our sphere of influence, to serving the people on the team. In fact, when we overemphasize the feelings and experience of the people within our organization to the neglect of our job, we are not being leaders at all—no matter how many people may line up behind us. Pied pipers woo people for the sake of their own gain. Spiritual leaders win followers for the sake of Christ and to further the kingdom of God.

What's Needed

What's needed, then, is a balanced model of leadership that holds together achieving the *right* kind of results and doing so in the *right* way. Effective leadership will be concerned both with producing high-quality results and with promoting a healthy, graceful, and stimulating work environment.

Results are important, because organizations and businesses are created to produce them; and leaders and staff are hired to achieve them. Measurable outcomes are helpful, because they allow us to evaluate the effectiveness of any endeavor that is worth our effort. At the same time, treating well and caring adequately for the people within our organization is also important, because each worker, serving in any position in the organization, deserves to be treated with respect. Furthermore, from a pragmatic point of view, a healthy, graceful, and stimulating work environment brings out the best in employees and group members, significantly supporting the long-term success of any enterprise.

Yet, the truth is, even if we know about all the components and dynamics of effective leadership, we may not know how to perform this balancing act or what action we can take to change our work environment. When I thought I did know the right thing to do, what I did at times felt awkward, forced, or insincere. Sometimes helping staff feel cared for seemed to require my acting or saying the right things or going through the right motions, even if I was thinking something quite different. I felt an internal tension that often produced mixed results at best.

On the other hand, leaders who overfocus on people or relationships may try hard to stay on track with goals, deadlines, and priorities, but find themselves overpowered by the demands of others. They may have a plan to produce great results, but feel in bondage to the feelings and wishes of everyone around them, without the freedom they need to meet job expectations. Their heart for others or need for others' approval may simply be too strong in the real world of everyday life at the office or in the committee.

So what's the answer to becoming truly more effective leaders?

It's not to try harder. That's exhausting.

It's also not to attempt to be "nicer." Even if that "works" by helping others to feel better about us, we will likely still be churning on the inside.

Pretending we are not disappointed, frustrated, angry, or annoyed doesn't work either. Despite our best attempts at self-control, our feelings usually have a way of seeping out. Comments that fail to hide a thinly veiled hostility and negative nonverbal communication can cause more negative results than straightforward talk about concerns and issues.

If you're a people pleaser, exerting your will to shut people out and focus on tasks isn't the answer either. Your heart won't be able to stand it, your unmet relationship needs will make you antsy or moody, and others around you will find an unhealthy way to get your attention anyway.

In short, just recognizing the value of leadership that balances concern for results and concern for people isn't the same as being an effective leader. Even trying our hardest to compensate for our tendencies to go to one extreme or the other is likely to fall short. Something more is necessary—something far deeper and more powerful.

To be the leaders God intends us to be and to lead in ways that honor God and bear the fruit God intends, what is needed is nothing short of personal transformation—a true inner change of heart, mind, and soul—that ultimately leads to a transformation of our leadership. Though many external factors may influence our effectiveness as leaders, it is the internal ones that we must come to grips with if we truly want to become the leaders we have been called to be.

Inner transformation begins with a willingness and commitment to do the hard work of personal and professional development. In the personal dimension of growth, we need to believe that as we become more whole people, our ability to lead will become both broader and deeper. We need to value developing emotionally, socially, psychologically, and spiritually, believing that as we grow as people, we will grow as leaders.

The professional dimension of growth is equally important. Periodically, someone will object to calling pastors or other Christian ministry leaders "professionals." Some fear weakening the prophetic voice of the Christian leader; others worry about contaminating the sacred nature of the calling. I, too, am deeply concerned that Christian leaders maintain a clear witness and a vibrant spirituality, but I am not afraid of the professional label. In fact, I welcome it, because to me it communicates a commitment to high standards, integrity, and skilled service. To reach our potential as leaders, we need to see ourselves as professionals, in the best sense of the word, and seek to grow in every way possible.

Then comes action. We need to roll up our sleeves, draw on available resources, and set aside the necessary time and energy to develop ourselves. We need to learn to do our jobs better, to acquire more knowledge, and to try new strategies and tactics. We need to do our own personal "work" to get healthier and to mature, and to develop whatever professional skills we can to excel in our jobs.

Yet professional growth goes beyond acquiring new information, skills, and methods. Inner transformation means a fundamental change in our mind-set, so that we truly think differently, and perceive God, others, our work, and ourselves in healthier and more constructive ways. It also involves a change in our heart, so that we increasingly become motivated by love.

The process of internal change is not the same for everyone. The potential catalysts may include formal education, inner healing, confession of sins and repentance, the discipline of being mentored, meaningful relationships, experiences with others, and psychotherapy. Inner transformation can come also from first making concrete changes in behavior, such as adjusting our operating policies and procedures, practicing new leadership styles, and reordering our priorities—provided that these changes are not gimmicks or furtive attempts to manipulate others.

Above all, the greatest potential contributor to personal and professional development is our own spiritual growth. As our relationship with God deepens and we learn to integrate our spiritual life and leadership more fully, we will begin to understand spiritual leadership in new ways. As we seek to lead in ways that focus on what God is doing in us and in the organization we serve, we will experience more of the abundant life than we imagined possible, and so will those who work with us.

Spirituality and Spiritual Transformation

A simple definition of spirituality is our sense of connection to God. For the purposes of this book, I am assuming a Christian frame of reference, based on New Testament teaching. God is our Creator, and we live because of the life God gives us (Acts 17:24-28). While God is distinct from his creatures, God is also present within believers through the Holy Spirit (Eph. 1:13). As human creations, we have a spiritual dimension that allows us to commune with our unseen Creator God, who is spirit (John 4:24). God's Spirit within us is what makes inner transformation possible and gives us the power to live godly lives (Gal. 5:16-25).

For many Christians, connection to God takes the form of a strong personal relationship with Christ. An informal survey I conducted among Christian leaders resulted in a number of definitions of spirituality that focused on Christ. One pastor said, "Spirituality is the pursuit of Christ, leading to a life like Christ's." A church historian, Mark Burrows of Andover Newton Theological Seminary, who has done extensive academic work on the subject, defines spirituality as a "lived experience and expression of Christian life."

Regardless of one's definition of spirituality, people have varying degrees of awareness of God and God's presence in their lives, from a vague sense of a life force within or around them to an intimate, personal relationship with God. The greater our sense of connection to God and the more that connection affects our life, the more vital our spirituality. Thus, vital spirituality refers to a strong sense of connection to God that significantly influences our thinking, feeling, and behavior.

Spiritual transformation involves inner changes that make our spiritual life more vital. All of us have a spiritual dimension to our lives, but we do not all experience spiritual transformation; and of those who experience spiritual transformation, not all experiences are the same. Yet from a biblical point of view, spiritual transformation is rooted in God's work in our life and involves many recognizable cognitive, emotional, and behavioral changes.

First, spiritual transformation includes an ongoing process of moving from a self-centered worldview and self-serving functioning to a God-centered perspective and devotion to serving God's purposes. For Christians, God-centered thinking and living lead to placing God (Father, Son, and Holy Spirit) at the center of one's life. God is the source of life. God redeems our life and provides the power to live out our God-given purpose in life. In more personal terms, spiritual transformation also deepens our awareness of God's love for us and increases our love for God. The greater our transformation, the more God's love permeates our senses, our thinking, and our way of living.

The paradox of spiritual transformation is that we serve our own best interests when we abandon self-serving thinking and behavior to serve God by following Christ. Jesus' startling words to his disciples illustrate the paradoxical nature of vital spirituality.[3] He says in effect that if we truly have our own best interests in mind, we will renounce our attempts to please and serve ourselves to follow him and serve the gospel. Mark summarized Jesus' teaching on the subject this way:

> [Jesus] called the crowd with his disciples, and said to them, "If any want to become my followers, let them deny themselves and take up their cross and follow me. For those who want to save their life will lose it, and those who lose their life for my sake, and for the sake of the gospel, will save it."
> Mark 8:34-35 NRSV

Mark, then, maintains that "life" is attainable only through a certain kind of response to Jesus and the gospel Jesus proclaimed: life comes to those who have faith in and are devoted to Jesus, evidenced by their renouncing the impulse to trust in and rule their own life and by following Jesus even to the point of suffering and death. The broader context of the

Gospel of Mark indicates that Jesus had in mind more than just saving their physical life; he was talking about a quality of life that begins in this life and extends into the next.[4]

For our purposes here, Jesus' main point is that the way to this quality of life begins with a right relationship with God. The alternative to gaining one's life Jesus' way is ultimately losing one's life—through attempts to gain it by promoting oneself and one's will alone, in isolation from an awareness of or devotion to God. Thus, the resolution of the paradox that we lose our life to find it is that the conflict is not between anti-self and pro-self; the conflict is living one's life out of a right relationship with God versus trying to go it alone without reliance on God.

John the Evangelist talked about vital spirituality as eternal life, a special quality of life produced by the Holy Spirit. We first experience it in the course of our natural life, and it extends into eternity. He begins to explain this concept by telling the story of Jesus and Nicodemus, in which Jesus taught that participation in the kingdom of God requires spiritual transformation; that is, being born of the Spirit.

> Jesus answered, "Very truly, I tell you, no one can enter the kingdom of God without being born of water and Spirit. What is born of the flesh is flesh, and what is born of the Spirit is spirit. Do not be astonished that I said to you, 'You must be born from above.' The wind blows where it chooses, and you hear the sound of it, but you do not know where it comes from or where it goes. So it is with everyone who is born of the Spirit."
>
> John 3:5-8 NRSV

In the same chapter, Jesus indicates that the spiritual birth he described to Nicodemus not only is produced by the Spirit; it comes about because of God's great love for humanity, which he demonstrated by giving his Son to save the world. The required human response to God's love and Jesus' sacrifice is faith, to which John alluded earlier in the Gospel when he described Jesus as the Lamb who takes away the sin of the world (John

1:29). By trusting in Christ, we may have an assurance of for-giveness of sins and freedom from fear of condemnation:

> For God so loved the world that he gave his only Son, so that everyone who believes in him may not perish but may have eternal life. Indeed, God did not send the Son into the world to condemn the world, but in order that the world might be saved through him.
>
> John 3:16-17 NRSV

From this one chapter, we can develop a definition: spiri-tual transformation includes recognizing God's loving initia-tive in Christ, experiencing a dynamic encounter with the Spirit of God, and having faith in Jesus as God's Son, who gave his life to save the world.

The apostle Paul's writings consistently affirm what Mark and John pointed to about the spiritual life, especially empha-sizing the transformative role of the Holy Spirit. Among many references, Paul describes the vital spiritual life as being set free from condemnation and the power of sin by the power of the Holy Spirit at work within those who are in relationship to Christ (Rom. 8:1-2). He sums up his teaching by saying, "For all who are led by the Spirit of God are children of God" (Rom. 8:14).

Late in the chapter Paul stresses an important quality of God's love for those who have faith in Jesus Christ: God's love is permanent and utterly reliable. He concludes:

> For I am convinced that neither death, nor life, nor angels, nor rulers, nor things present, nor things to come, nor pow-ers, nor height, nor depth, nor anything else in all creation will be able to separate us from the love of God in Christ Jesus our Lord.
>
> Romans 8:38-39 NRSV

God's part in our spiritual transformation is to provide for-giveness and eternal life through our faith in Jesus Christ and the activity of the Holy Spirit in our life. Our part in cultivat-ing our spiritual life includes an appropriate response to all that God provides. We begin with faith and move to putting our life at the complete disposal of God to serve God's will in every way possible. Paul describes this response as offering ourselves as a "living sacrifice" and renewing our minds that we may be transformed:

> I appeal to you therefore, brothers and sisters, by the mercies of God, to present your bodies as a living sacrifice, holy and acceptable to God, which is your spiritual worship. Do not be conformed to this world, but be transformed by the renewing of your minds, so that you may discern what is the will of God—what is good and acceptable and perfect.
>
> Romans 12:1-2 NRSV

Spiritual transformation also includes learning to let the Holy Spirit produce certain desirable qualities within us and in our relationships. Paul depicts this phenomenon as "walking by the Spirit"; he lists many of the attributes of the Spirit-led person in his letter to the Galatians:

> Live by the Spirit, I say, and do not gratify the desires of the flesh. . . . The fruit of the Spirit is love, joy, peace, patience, kindness, generosity, faithfulness, gentleness, and self-control. There is no law against such things. . . . If we live by the Spirit, let us also be guided by the Spirit.
>
> Galatians 5:16, 22-23, 25 NRSV

Finally, transformative spiritual experiences usually come with a significant emotional response. Peter describes the joy, hope, and love that faith produce:

> Blessed be the God and Father of our Lord Jesus Christ! By his great mercy he has given us a new birth into a *living hope* through the resurrection of Jesus Christ from the dead, and into an inheritance that is imperishable, undefiled, and unfading, kept in heaven for you. . . . In this you *rejoice*, even if now for a little while you have had to suffer various trials. . . . Although you have not seen him, you *love* him;

and even though you do not see him now, *you believe in him and rejoice with an indescribable and glorious joy*, for you are receiving the outcome of your *faith*, the salvation of your souls.

1 Peter 1:3, 6, 8-9 NRSV, emphasis added

In sum, as the example and teaching of Jesus and various biblical writers affirm, spiritual transformation involves many cognitive, emotional, and behavioral changes in the life of a believer. God's loving and gracious activity leads us to embrace and pursue an intimate, loving relationship with God the Father, Son, and Holy Spirit. As we increasingly grasp the magnitude of God's grace, we grow in our gratitude and joyful appreciation for all God has done for us. We increasingly move from a self-centered to a God-centered orientation, making significant changes in our perspective and priorities. As the Holy Spirit gains greater influence within us, we become Spirit-led people who live out our calling in life by God's leading and power. We are increasingly changed from the inside out, experiencing faith, hope, love, and other fruits of the Spirit.

Spiritual Leadership

Spiritual leadership is something we offer to others when we consciously draw on God as the wellspring for our life and leadership. Spiritual leaders, like all spiritually vital individuals, seek to be continually transformed through their relationship to God. In addition, spiritual leaders use their own faith, experience, and knowledge of spiritual principles and practices, as well as their position of leadership, to influence their workplace spiritually.

As the context permits, spiritual leaders also consciously foster connection to and reliance on God among board members, staff, and all stakeholders and beneficiaries of the organization, company, or ministry. They seek to cultivate a spiritually rich environment—not to promote doctrine but to catalyze team members to seek God and God's will together. In short, spiritual leaders, in every way possible within the boundaries of their leadership context, seek the Holy Spirit's leading for themselves and for their team members as they work together. They are Spirit-led leaders, who seek to pilot Spirit-led teams and organizations.

Congregations, institutions, co-workers, and staff members are often longing for Spirit-led leaders to bring spiritual vitality into the workplace, whether they realize it or not. They want greater depth of wisdom, discernment, and spiritual sensitivity in their leaders. They need help to avoid losing their souls as they attempt to navigate a fast-paced, high-pressure, performance-oriented culture that has an insatiable appetite for results. They want their experience as workers to match the values their organization espouses to customers, donors, or congregation members. They want to be fully valued as contributing members of the body of Christ, and treated respectfully as spiritually gifted individuals.

However, while the value of spiritual leadership is evident, few leaders seem to grasp what is needed, let alone have the ability to provide it. They may feel inadequate or stymied in their efforts to be spiritual leaders. They may be unsure how to integrate spiritual emphases with corporate goals and objectives. A religiously diverse staff may pose challenges that seem insurmountable or limiting to a leader's ability to promote vital spirituality in the workplace. Leaders may not be able to get past their own performance- and results-oriented mentality. They also may not see how they can both show care and compassion for those they lead *and* produce the results expected of them. They may not know how to pursue a deeper spiritual life or how to let their leadership be transformed by it, let alone how to foster a richer spiritual environment among their co-workers. For whatever reasons, a vacuum of effective spiritual leadership exists in many churches and organizations today.

The Way Forward

Disillusioned leaders, burned-out clergy, weary executives, and demoralized staff members, not to mention disenchanted parishioners and a disaffected public at large, call for change. Many painful and frustrating experiences finally forced me to recognize the magnitude of this need.

The solution is spiritual leadership by Spirit-led leaders. Such leaders will cultivate a vital personal relationship to God that they consciously seek to integrate with their leadership, leading to a transformation of themselves and their leadership.

I now accept that many of the problems I was having as a leader, particularly in my role as a program director and most recently as executive director of a nonprofit organization, were due to a false dichotomy in my mind between administrative leadership—vision casting, strategic planning, managing, or coordinating others—and spiritual leadership, which I saw as a combination of supportive pastoral ministry to staff, preaching, teaching, and prayer. When I didn't know how to integrate these two dimensions of leadership, or when my own preoccupation with results undermined my spiritual and relational sensitivities and priorities, my effectiveness as a leader suffered. Many times I blamed staff or volunteers for some lack I perceived in them. Now I realize that I was often the main problem.

I needed to mature and deepen spiritually and learn to think and act differently as a leader. I had to focus far more on the process of leadership and somewhat less on my desired outcomes. I discovered that it was better to let God lead and work in me, among the team members and in the ministry, than to try to make things happen by the force of my own will. I needed to make certain changes in my thinking and in how I guided the organization to make decisions and conduct business.

Three significant shifts in my heart, mind, and practice particularly have helped me to become a more effective organizational leader. Each relates to my own spiritual life or how I understood the connection between spirituality and leadership.

The first life-changing experience came from a profound encounter I had with the grace of God. I came to a new understanding of myself as a precious child of God—loved, forgiven, and called by God to serve Christ with certain gifts and abilities I had been given. This mental shift allowed me to rest in God's love and grace in a new way, which set me free from the guilt and shame that were producing an insidious, driving impulse to achieve in order to feel good about myself. I still work hard, but now I do so much more from a desire to participate in God's activity in the world.

My experience with the grace of God not only began to transform my self-image; it also significantly influenced the way I related to my wife, my children, and other people in general. At times my old shame-based, performance-oriented thinking creeps back, wreaking havoc on my own peace of mind and on relationships with others. Yet, an enduring shift has taken place. Grace is increasingly fundamental, not only to my relationship with God but also to every other aspect of my personal life and leadership.

The second significant change resulted from a fresh understanding of leadership as an outgrowth of my spiritual life. The more I developed a vision for my own spiritual growth and for the integration of my spiritual life and leadership, the less I saw a division between administrative leadership and spiritual leadership, and the less they seemed opposed to one another. In fact, now I see my spiritual life and spiritual leadership as the central integrating forces of every aspect of my organizational leadership.

The third paradigm shift came when I began to understand spiritual leadership as leading the team as a whole, rather than trying to minister to individual staff members in a pastoral sort of role. There was just too much tension between competing instincts for me to minister effectively to staff one to one on a regular basis.

On the one hand, in my unofficial, self-designated role as "pastor" to staff members within our organization, I wanted to encourage them to grow in their relationship to God and to help them cope with disappointment, discouragement, and even failure in their work. On the other hand, as supervisor, I wanted to challenge them to set high standards and hold themselves accountable; I didn't want to take no for an answer, and I wanted our work relationships to focus on the tasks at hand and corporate goals.

Not knowing how to resolve these two competing impulses, I experienced a host of conflicting feelings, leading others to feel confused and distressed at times as well. For example, I felt joy when I was able to encourage or nurture a staff member, but then uncomfortable and awkward when I had to turn around and hold him or her accountable in the next moment. I felt frustrated if staff members didn't want me to relate to them in a pastoral way, when I sensed I had something to offer them spiritually. And I felt frustrated if they did want support or spiritual nurture when I thought my higher priority was to address performance issues. I felt guilty when I was more concerned about the results of their work than the state of their spiritual life, and guilty when we spent time discussing meaningful spiritual issues instead of attending to job performance.

I have found that my administrative and spiritual leadership roles conflict far less often since I changed my approach to spiritual leadership. Now, instead of trying to be a pastor to each individual, I seek to be the spiritual leader for the team as a whole.

I have come to believe that for administrators to focus on supervisory issues with staff who report directly to them does not mean that they cannot serve as spiritual leaders, nor does it mean that they should confine their attention to results and performance. Rather than trying to be a pastor or spiritual guide to individual staff members, they can serve as spiritual leaders of their work group or team by drawing on their own spiritual life as they lead. They can offer their leadership and management as deeply spiritual people who actively incorporate spiritual principles and practices into every aspect of their work as members of a group or team of co-workers.

In general, then, leaders should not try to be the primary, personal pastor or spiritual caregiver for someone they supervise. While on rare occasions such a dual role—pastor and supervisor—may work, usually a supervisor's need to focus on performance will conflict with the desire of the pastor to encourage and nurture. It is better for both the staff member and the supervisor when the staff member has solid spiritual and pastoral resources outside of the workplace. The ideal is for each worker to come to work as "filled up" as possible, as a whole person, eager and ready to serve Christ and the mission of the organization with his or her co-workers and boss.

The principle of finding pastoral and spiritual support from someone other than one's boss is applicable to staff members of churches as well. If an employee's supervisor is one of the pastors, a conflict of interest will arise at some point for everyone involved, limiting the quality of supervision, the pastoral guidance and support, or both. A good option for people who are both members and employees of a congregation is to find someone outside their church to meet their pastoral and spiritual needs. Pastors of other churches, spiritual directors, or chaplains in the area might be willing to serve in a supportive role.

These three shifts—from performance-based to grace-based living and leading, from dichotomous to integrated thinking about organizational and spiritual leadership, and from efforts to serve as pastor to individual staff members to serving as spiritual leader of the organization as a whole—have taken me a long way from my first attempts to be an effective leader. I am still results-oriented, but I have abandoned my force-it-to-happen style of leadership and compartmentalized thinking about leadership and spirituality. My greatest priority is cultivating my own spiritual life and leading from a strong spiritual frame of reference.

The results I now value more than any other are those that have a significant spiritual dimension. They are built on a foundation of grace and grow out of the Holy Spirit's work in my own life and the gifts given to me and to others with whom I work. I feel a tremendous sense of satisfaction when we reach corporate goals, but equally important to me are the spiritual quality of the work environment and the methods used to achieve results.

The Spirit-Led Leader

Countless books and seminars are available to help leaders become better visionaries, more effective managers, more psychologically self-aware persons, better speakers and communicators, and more efficient stewards of time and resources. What is needed is biblically grounded, experientially validated material to help Christian leaders to deepen their own spiritual lives and to lead from a place of greater spiritual depth. Encouraging and helping leaders to become effective spiritual leaders is what *The Spirit-Led Leader* is about.

This book begins in chapter 1 by creating a new vision for spiritual leadership. Chapters 2 and 3 focus on how leaders can experience the grace of God in life-changing ways and can develop a deeper spiritual life. Chapters 4 through 8 focus on ways to integrate one's spiritual life and leadership, so that ultimately every aspect of one's leadership will be spiritual at its core. The final chapter addresses the real heart of spiritual leadership—experiencing and expressing the grace of God.

Each chapter explores a key leadership practice under the heading "What's Needed." A practice is something for leaders to do. Later in each chapter, a corresponding soul principle is discussed in the section "What's Real." The principle supports or informs the practice, and leaders will want to think and pray about how to incorporate it further into their spiritual life and leadership.[5]

Every chapter also has a section called "Here's Help," which includes ideas or exercises to help readers integrate the practice and principle discussed in the chapter in their life and leadership. The brief final section of each chapter offers "Something to Think About." Here you will find suggestions for further reflection. You can work through the material of the last two sections of each chapter alone, with professional peers, or with co-workers. I recommend taking time to think, journal, and pray about the practice and principle first individually and then with your leadership team.

The Spirit-Led Leader is designed for pastors, executives, administrators, managers, coordinators, and all who see themselves as leaders who want to fulfill their God-given purpose as God intends. The book is for those who want to see "results" but who are learning to care just as deeply about who they are and how they lead as they care about what they produce and accomplish. It is for those who want to experience the abundant life that God intends for them and who want to see their organizations become what God envisions.

At heart, this book is about hope.

There is hope for those who want to produce excellent results that further the kingdom of God and who want to do so as effective spiritual leaders. There is also hope for the many churches and organizations that are longing for vital spiritual leadership.

By God's grace, spiritual transformation and spiritual leadership are always possibilities. As leaders, we will always be flawed and limited, but hope for change and growth continually exists, so long as God is active in our lives and we are willing to do our part. That's what the good news of God's grace is all about—God's work in our lives for good through faith in Jesus Christ and the power of the Holy Spirit.

THE VISION

Leadership Practice
Envision your leadership flowing out of a deep spiritual life.

Soul Principle
Fruitfulness in leadership requires the work of
God in and through us.

In our postmodern, experience-oriented, relational culture, people want those who lead them to have more than knowledge and skills. Many parishioners, staff members, and students are longing for greater authenticity, integrity, and depth from their pastors, organizational heads, supervisors, mentors, and teachers. Many want their leaders to possess certain personal qualities in addition to professional competence. Whether or not they can articulate it, they are looking for a spiritual vitality that influences every aspect of leaders' lives, including how they think, treat others, and conduct themselves as leaders.

For example, when a pastor gets up to preach, parishioners are listening for how the preacher has struggled to live out his or her teaching within a family, neighborhood, and work situation. When leaders cast visions and lead the charge, staff members want to feel valued and appreciated, and followers want leaders to be honest, trustworthy, and faithful. Many want those who hold a place of authority to have good hearts as well as good heads. We want them to get the job done, but we want them also to be loving and caring people, as well as people of mental substance and wisdom.

Experts on leadership—such as Jim Collins, author of a best-selling analysis of companies that have gone from "good to great" over the past century—have come to a similar conclusion: excellent leaders are more than masters at achieving results; they have outstanding personal attributes as well.[1] These qualities are often summed up as personal character, a distinguishing mark of the highest level of leadership. Many students of leadership believe that what is even more important is the source of these attributes: a vital spiritual life.[2]

C. Michael Thompson, who heads a private consulting practice focusing on organizational and individual leadership development, argues that acting from a solid spiritual base is the most important dimension of effective leadership. In essence, he maintains that a vital spirituality is key to the quality and the character of anyone, especially the leader:

> A strong inner life plays a key and indispensable role in personal growth and development. And such personal growth, with the emotional, attitudinal, and behavioral changes it produces, is not simply a helpful adjunct to organizational leadership these days—it is its essence. The logic is simply this: of the literally hundreds of skills, competencies, traits, characteristics, and qualities used in the literature to define leadership, those that are most essential in the fluid and chaotic reality of the world today are in fact the outer fruits of that devoted inner life.[3]

Why do Thompson and others stress the inner life? Because effective leaders need to draw from a deep well within to handle shifting and complex demands, and to do so in ways that inspire those they lead. Leaders need more than knowledge and expertise. They need insight, understanding, and an ability to show as well as proclaim the way. Followers want to *experience* the wisdom of leaders in their relationship with them, and not just hear it from them or read about it.

As more people in our culture come to recognize the high value of spiritual vitality in leaders, it is not surprising that board directors, elders and deacons, church members, other worshipers, and staff are all seeking leaders who have spiritual depth as well as professional competence. That is, they are looking for high-quality leaders who can produce excellent corporate or ministry outcomes *and* who embody and live out spiritual vibrancy in their own devotional life, work relationships, and treatment of others. Whether or not they can put their expectations into words like these, they want leaders who have experienced what they are preaching, teaching, and promoting, and who draw from a deep well of personal spirituality.

Some readers might sarcastically object, "But Jesus isn't available! Why hold up an ideal that only Jesus could fulfill?" Indeed, many individuals and groups have unrealistic expectations for their leaders, putting unfair and unhealthy demands on them. Nonetheless, even if some people's expectations exceed what is reasonable, that failing doesn't invalidate their longing, values, and concerns. The lack of realism in the high expectations of search committees doesn't invalidate the tremendous need for strong, spiritually mature leaders in our executive offices, pulpits, parachurch agencies, and boardrooms.

Forget the expectations of others for a moment. What are your own goals for your spiritual life and for the spiritual quality of your leadership? Too often, we leaders react to the expectations and demands of others either by frantically scrambling to meet them or by defensively explaining why we can't or won't. Instead, let's proactively create our own vision for leadership and set our own goals for the person we want to become, how we want to relate to God, and how we want to lead.

Do you have a vision for your spiritual life and leadership?

What's Needed

Envision your leadership flowing out of a deep spiritual life.

Stories abound of great leaders who may be effective preachers, teachers, or entrepreneurs, but who for one reason or another do not provide excellent spiritual leadership within their organizations. By the grace of God, they may contribute to furthering the kingdom of God, but something significant is missing in their leadership.

Some leaders are overfocused on results. They are eager to marshal the resources of their organization to accomplish great outcomes, but they lack the vision or the ability to apply spiritual principles to their work relationships. They may routinely alienate or neglect staff members, or frustrate and discourage them with unrealistic expectations. They may be natural visionaries and leaders but fail to treat staff in ways that match the values and beliefs they promote in public. They may have a deep personal faith, but one that is not integrated with their leadership in ways that enhance the workplace or the lives and ministries of co-workers.

Conversely, many of us know caring pastors, executives, or managers—people in leadership positions—who relate effectively to individuals, handle personnel issues with sensitivity, or radiate a spiritual vitality, but who lack the ability to move a ministry forward. They may have a vision for growth and practical knowledge of how the church or organization could expand the scope of its ministry, yet fear conflict or find themselves overwhelmed by difficult issues that must be dealt with for the sake of the whole team. They can't lead effectively, either because they lack the leadership ability or are too eager to please people.

Still other leaders may be highly influential in a community but neither produce superior long-term results in their ministries nor work well with their staff. These individuals may serve effectively on denominational or ecumenical task forces, as valued public speakers, committee members or authors, or in some other broader context, but not lead well within their own organizations. Though appreciated by other professionals, they do not function meaningfully among their co-workers and staff members as a team leader, spiritual mentor, caring supervisor, or in any other capacity needed to help their organization fulfill its mission effectively.

Whatever the reasons that some leaders fail to lead well, what's needed is usually more than shoring up shortcomings or addressing imbalances in leadership style. Achieving results, connecting meaningfully with people, and finding opportunities to influence others are all natural motivations for leaders, but none of them provide the right basis for Christian leadership.

Rather, Christian leaders need to be transformed from the inside out by fully integrating their spiritual life and leadership. Transformed leaders will be deeply spiritual people who seek to lead from a spiritual vitality that propels them into leadership roles, responsibilities, relationships, and opportunities. Such leaders will seek top-quality results, affiliate with others in meaningful ways, and become people of influence— but all for the right reasons; that is, because they are devoted to serving God's purposes, they are seeking to be good stewards of their spiritual gifts, they are called to leadership, they are being transformed inwardly, and they are empowered by God to serve effectively.

How do we become such leaders?

The transformation of our leadership begins with a vision for effective spiritual leadership and requires drawing on spiritual practices and principles that help us to pursue the vision.[4] Visions do not describe present reality. They portray something that can be imagined and is desired but has not yet come to pass. Visions are not just for so-called visionaries, who have a special knack or gift for creating great visions for themselves or their organizations. They are for anyone who wants to experience a better life, relationship, job, church, or organization—and who can imagine what "better" might mean in this context.

Consider a well-known analogy from the physical world. Mount Everest has long been the ultimate goal for serious mountain climbers. To reach the summit, a would-be climber needs months of preparation, conditioning, and training. However, the venture does not begin with the difficult advance work. It begins with a vision. The climber imagines standing atop the world's highest peak, beholding a magnificent view, and enjoying a tremendous sense of accomplishment. It's the vision, not the thought of the arduous and dangerous climb, that inspires and motivates the adventure.

Envisioning your leadership as flowing out of a deep spiritual life means picturing yourself as a highly effective spiritual leader. This vision includes seeing yourself as possessing an intimate and nourishing relationship with God that overflows into and transforms every aspect of your life and leadership. You can imagine God's power working through you to accomplish significant results, to help you relate well and effectively with team members and other staff, and to increase your influence to include everyone God has in mind to benefit from your leadership.

Of course, a host of factors will affect your ability to realize such a vision, including some that are outside your control. Your leadership may not flourish the way you imagine for any number of reasons, some discernible and some obscure. Nevertheless, we are not talking here about the things you cannot change or affect, but about what you *can* do—and that begins with creating and holding a biblically sound, God-inspired vision for your leadership. You will have plenty of opportunities to be "realistic" about your limits and challenges on a day-to-day basis, but ultimate success in leadership depends on holding firmly to the vision.[5]

We need also to come to grips with what drives us to lead in the ways we do and how we measure success.[6] The right vision will help us answer these questions. Will we evaluate our leadership primarily by our ability to achieve results and accomplish corporate goals? Will we be concerned primarily with what people think of us or how well others like us? Will we pay the most attention to the size of our sphere of influence or who's taking notice of what we say or do? Or will we examine the degree to which our leadership flows out of a vital spiritual life, governed and empowered by God for the sake of Christ and his kingdom?

As leaders, we will always care about the results, the people, and the extent of our influence in the work we do. It's appropriate for us to have goals and to want good things to come from our labor. However, what undermines our effectiveness as spiritual leaders is focusing on the results, the people, and our influence as motivating forces in our life, instead of fixing our gaze on God's vision for our relationship with him and our leadership as an outgrowth of what God is doing in us and through us.

Start with the right vision, even if you don't know how you are going to realize it. Hold to that vision through the ups and downs of life, even when you feel inadequate or stymied in your efforts. Doggedly pursue it, and see what happens when you keep your eye on what God intends for you as a spiritual leader.

What's Real

Fruitfulness in leadership requires the work of God in and through us.

An important soul principle underlies the practice of envisioning your leadership as flowing in transformative ways out of a deep spiritual life. Fruitfulness in leadership requires the work of God in and through us. That is, the results that serve God's purposes and bring honor to God will be infused with God's presence, power, and character. Thus, focusing on God not only leads us to the right vision for leadership; it is absolutely necessary if we want to succeed by God's definition of success.

By contrast, any attempt to lead that relies solely on our own intelligence, wisdom, will power, personality, or efforts will be driven by ego, self-centeredness, or unhealthy needs and impulses. We may still produce impressive results, but an essential quality will be missing. For example, we may receive the honor instead of God. Others may become dependent on us rather than on Christ. Our organizations may flourish as enterprises or institutions, but they may fail to fulfill God's intentions for them.

What can be confusing is that we know we are supposed to rely on God, yet we are sure that we need to rely on ourselves as well. God has given each of us a certain intelligence; we have learned a lot in school and gained wisdom from experience; we have natural abilities and spiritual gifts that others appreciate; and we know that working hard does make a difference. Without a doubt, each of these dimensions of leadership is important to our success as a leader. However, the confusion about whom or what we are to rely on can be greatly reduced when we understand the difference between the source of our power and the resources available to us.

In Christian ministry, or in any work we do with the intention of honoring and serving Christ, God is the source of any fruitful endeavor that has lasting spiritual benefit to others. All that we bring to our work are resources we draw on as we participate in what God is doing through us. Though in practical terms it may be impossible at times to differentiate clearly between what God is doing and what we are doing, such an analysis is not the point. Our perspective and practice are what matter here: Do we think that our leadership is about our accomplishments or about what God is doing through us? Do we constantly push ourselves to try harder, or have we learned to slow down enough to seek consciously to draw on God's presence, power, and leading?

Our dependence on God's working is what makes the integration of our spiritual life and our leadership so critical. We cannot lead as an outgrowth of God's Spirit working in us if we relegate spirituality to our private life or to one dimension among many in our leadership. Such compartmentalization will guarantee that much of our work is based on something other than God's movement in us. We may find ourselves relying on our own ingenuity, philosophy of leadership, management paradigms, and hard work; on marketing, sales, or fund-raising strategies; and on any number of other *tools* for leadership that are inadequate *bases* for leadership. Only one base is adequate for Christian leadership—a vital spiritual life in which God is transforming us as individuals, and is leading and working through us as leaders.

To lead with excellence and to be a deeply spiritual person who seeks to cultivate a rich spiritual environment within the workplace are not competing enterprises. To think that these are opposed to one another creates a false dichotomy. In fact, until our leadership and spiritual life are thoroughly integrated, our ability to lead will suffer and we will experience many unnecessary and counterproductive conflicts.

If we are motivated mostly by results, we may drive people to accomplish our will, rather than lead a team to fulfill a God-given mission together. If we are motivated by the desire to be liked or approved of by people, we may lose sight of the mission in order to please others. If we are motivated largely by our desire to become people of influence, we may neglect both the mission of the organization and the people working within it to further our own reputation or to satisfy our ambition. In each case, misplaced priorities and values will lead to conflicts within us and with others. When our motivation for leading springs from our own desires rather than from God's working in us, it is only a matter of time before we will experience resentful staff, critical board members, tension, frustration, disappointment, and a host of other difficult and draining reactions.

In one way or another, all of these conflicts result from establishing our leadership on a faulty base, neglecting to integrate fully our faith and spiritual life with our leadership theory and practice. We fail to connect what we say we believe as Christians with how we go about leading others. We trust in the grace of God for our salvation and devote ourselves to serving Christ and the work of his kingdom but wind up pursuing our own agendas or trying to accomplish great things for God in our own strength.

To integrate our spiritual life and our leadership means to adopt a mind-set and "heart-set" that are congruent with the good news of the Christian faith. We will rejoice in the un-merited grace of God for ourselves as sinners, rest in the suffi-ciency of Christ's work for our standing with God, and rely on the work of the Holy Spirit for fruitfulness in ministry. In other words, our leadership will be built upon a solid foundation of God's work in our life; we will thus be freed from thinking that we have to achieve sufficient results, please the right people, or gain power in a certain sphere of influence to feel good about ourselves.

The less we feel the need to strive and strain to prove to others or to ourselves that we are lovable, valuable people, the more we will be free to serve Christ's purposes in our leader-ship. Instead of being slaves to producing results, pleasing people, or expanding our power or sphere of influence, we can look to the Holy Spirit to work through us to lead the team in the pursuit of God's agenda.

Objective and subjective measures are, to be sure, still rel-evant for evaluating our effectiveness as leaders; we need to submit both to self-examination and to a process of critique by others if we are to grow professionally; and the degree of power and influence that others grant us may be an indica-tion of our effectiveness. Nevertheless, our starting place for Christian leadership needs to be a well-grounded spiritual life that is congruent with the teaching of the gospel—in head, heart, action, and experience with God. As our spiritual life increasingly becomes the basis and driving force of our lead-ership, and as we use our Spirit-endowed gifts faithfully, our ministry as leaders will be fruitful—in God's timing, according to God's will, and as a result of God's working in and through us.

Of course, we can integrate our spiritual life and our lead-ership effectively only if we have a spiritual life. Our spiritual-ity needs to be firmly rooted in the good news of God's grace, not just intellectually but emotionally and experientially as well. On the thinking side of our humanity, our spiritual life will become more meaningful as we increasingly let our faith influence our worldview and mind-set in every aspect of our

life. On the feeling side, our spiritual life will gain strength
and intensity the more we let ourselves feel gratitude for God's
love, sorrow for sins, the joy of forgiveness, and the whole
range of human emotions that flow from grasping the meaning of faith, biblical teaching, and Christian doctrines. Experientially, our spiritual life deepens as we encounter God in
worship, in nature, in Scripture, or in any other aspect of life
that brings us to an awareness of God's presence and connection to us.

Furthermore, if we are to handle the demands of leadership, we can't afford to be complacent about our spiritual life
or satisfied with the status quo in our relationship with God.
We need to cultivate our relationship with God and to experience drawing on God's Spirit in leadership if we are to serve
most effectively. For example, leaders often need wisdom and
a special spiritual sensitivity to discern an organization's or
community's direction, or to determine how to handle difficult issues. Others look to leaders to show them the way, as
well as to teach them how to relate to God and how to draw
upon their relationship with God for strength and help.

Our spiritual depth as leaders sets the tone within our organization and produces richer and more meaningful relationships with co-workers and others. The more we know and
experience God, and the more our leadership is rooted in our
relationship with God, the more we will be at peace about our
life and work. The more we are at peace within ourselves, the
more we can be genuinely at peace with others. Even when
we must confront troubling issues, our inner peace and firm
spiritual grounding equip us to handle these conflicts and
challenges more constructively than we might otherwise.
Sometimes, however, the call to "go deeper" spiritually feels
overwhelming. We may not even know what it means, let alone
how to do it.

First, "going deeper spiritually" means going beyond holding orthodox beliefs and observing appropriate behaviors.
Spiritual depth also includes a growing ability to listen to God
and to experience God in ways that transform us. It involves
pursuing greater intimacy with God and becoming more at

ease with being led by the Spirit in every aspect of our life and leadership. Spiritual transformation is multidimensional, too. We experience greater knowledge, richer feelings, a better sense of connection to God, and more fruitful and meaningful service. The more holistic and thorough our spiritual transformation, the more every aspect of our being will be affected. To oversimplify, if we think about our spiritual life in terms of head, heart, soul, and body, then spiritual transformation includes thinking new thoughts about God, ourselves, and others; feeling all of the powerful and wonderful feelings that come from being in a right relationship with God; experiencing God in the course of daily life; and behaving in more godly ways that serve others well—all as an outgrowth of a deepening and growing relationship with God.[7]

Second, we must remember that God does not expect us to go deeper by our own strength. In the New Testament, believers are frequently called to transform their thinking and living, but the assumption is always that change is made possible by God's work within the believer. For example, the Apostle Paul urged the Christians in Philippi to "work out [their] salvation," by which he meant that they needed to order their lives in ways that flowed logically from having a Christian faith. Yet, he coupled his exhortation with an affirmation that God is the one who gives the desire, will, and ability to live in ways that please God. Paul says, "Therefore, my beloved, . . . work out your own salvation with fear and trembling; for it is God who is at work in you, enabling you both to will and to work for his good pleasure" (Phil. 2:12-13 NRSV). Spiritual growth in all its dimensions is not simply the product of our own efforts. Despite the steps we can take to enrich our spiritual life (the focus of chapters 2 and 3), God is the true source of spiritual vitality and life transformation. Spiritual transformation is the calling of all Christians, but God's work within us is the key.

Jesus Christ expressed this principle in different words in the well-known analogy of the vine and the branches (John 15:1-8). As the vine, Jesus provides the nourishment needed for us, the branches, to bear fruit. Only by maintaining this intimate, ongoing connection to him—above all else, being transformed into people of love—can we expect to bear fruit in our life and ministries. Our spiritual vitality and depth are what enable us truly to love one another and to imitate Jesus by sacrificially serving others (John 15:12-13).

The apostle Paul talked also about the role of God's Spirit in equipping and enabling the body of Christ, including its leaders. For example, in teaching how God works through individuals in various ways to meet the needs of the entire congregation, Paul wrote, "Now there are varieties of gifts, but the same Spirit; and there are varieties of services, but the same Lord; and there are varieties of activities, but it is the same God who activates all of them in everyone. To each is given the manifestation of the Spirit for the common good" (1 Cor. 12:4-7 NRSV).

These three passages, among many others in the New Testament, clearly teach that God the Father, Son, and Holy Spirit is the primary force behind our spiritual vitality, transformation, and ministry. Those particularly called to leadership are to lead out of a meaningful connection to God. We are to make every effort to be spiritually well grounded, to grow, and to model the values and principles we espouse; but we must rely on God to transform us and to make us effective spiritual leaders. That's the vision.

Here's Help

As we seek to build an appropriate, biblically based vision for spiritual leadership, biblical figures are obvious resources for us. We each have our own calling, but we can learn from the examples of others to help us to envision the future reality of our own Spirit-led and Spirit-empowered leadership.

Such Old Testament leaders as Abraham, Joseph, Moses, Gideon, Deborah, and David provide excellent examples of devotion to God's will, trust in God, and reliance on God's leading and power for effective leadership. In the New Testament, Peter and Paul stand out as spiritual leaders who rely on visions, dreams, and the power of the Holy Spirit to know how to lead or to serve more effectively.[8] Above all, Jesus is the greatest biblical example of a spiritual leader, one who led out of a vital connection to and relationship with God, and whose spiritual life was thoroughly integrated with his leadership.

Jesus Models Spiritual Leadership

Jesus embodied what he asked of his disciples and what he hoped would develop in their lives: loving devotion to God, an active prayer life, service to others, and action based on faith. He was submissive to God's will, giving of himself sacrificially in obedience to God's purpose for his life. The way he treated the populace at large matched how he treated his disciples—with high expectations, solid teaching, personal investment in their lives, grace, mercy, and love. When Jesus was abrupt or sharp with the Pharisees or his disciples, he seems to have had a pedagogical purpose. A point needed to be made. At that moment, expressing the truth was more important than coddling them. Nevertheless, Jesus is best known as a friend to sinners, consistently gracious, forgiving, and supportive of his co-workers and associates.

Jesus' relationship with God was authentic. On the one hand, his love for his *Abba* (Aramaic for "Father") was independent of his role as a leader among people. That is, he didn't develop his relationship with his father to help him become a better preacher, teacher, or healer. Rather, he maintained a strong connection to God because he placed a higher value on his relationship with his father than on anything else. Yet on the other hand, Jesus' spiritual life was integral to his role as leader among people. He sought God's guidance in choosing his disciples and asked God in the garden of Gethsemane for strength to fulfill his mission and purpose. Jesus faced imposing challenges from opponents; he was frustrated by the immaturity of his disciples; he suffered unjustly at the hands of others. Still, he responded appropriately and effectively in situation after situation, no doubt because of the deep connection he actively cultivated with God the Father.

As we seek to create our own visions for spiritual leadership, Jesus provides an example to us of great spiritual depth and integrity that we can emulate. He valued his connection to God above all else. He grounded his own life and sense of self in his devoted personal relationship with his Father. His leadership and ministry grew out of that intimate and vital connection.[9]

Integrating Your Spiritual Life and Leadership

Another tool for developing a better-integrated vision for your spiritual leadership is reflecting on your own experience and discussing that vision with others. The following is a short exercise that you can do on your own for personal reflection and then use with staff members, a leadership team, or a group of professional peers. It is designed to help participants think about the relationship between their spiritual life and leadership—both their experience and their vision for the future.

After reading this chapter, write your response to the reflection questions below in the space provided or on three-by-five-inch cards. In a group setting, the exercise may be done in triads. The facilitator of the process can assign individuals to groups or let them self-select. Within the triads, each group member assumes one of three roles: speaker, listener, or observer. At the end of the exercise, participants may switch roles and go through the process a second and a third time.

Questions for Reflection

1. How have I experienced tension between my spiritual life and my leadership role and responsibilities?

2. How would I be different as a leader if my spiritual life flowed more freely and fully into my leadership daily?

Instructions for Triads (10 minutes)

Four minutes: Speaker shares with listener his or her responses to the reflection questions. Observer keeps time and pays attention to nonverbal communication and any dynamics that emerge between speaker and listener.

Four minutes: Listener helps speaker process thoughts and experiences by asking clarifying questions. Listener's role is not to introduce his or her own opinions or to pry, but to ask for further clarification of ideas and feelings speaker has shared. Observer keeps time and notices any dynamics that emerge during the interaction between speaker and listener.

Two minutes: Observer shares what he or she has seen, heard, thought, wondered about, or felt while observing speaker and listener.

Option: Switch roles and repeat the process until each person has had the opportunity to play each role.

Reflection on the Exercise

Take a minute to jot down a reflection on your experience(s) in the triad exercise. Then compare notes with others in your group. What struck you as significant?

- As speaker . . .

- As listener . . .

- As observer . . .

Going Deeper

This exercise has a secondary goal. The first is to give you an opportunity to identify and clarify both your own experience of and vision for integrating your spiritual life and leadership to become a spiritual leader. The second is to help participants become more aware that each of these three perspectives—speaking, listening, and observing—provides opportunities to gather important but different insights into spiritual leadership.

To serve most effectively as spiritual leaders, we must develop our abilities to speak, listen, and observe. We will return to this idea in chapters that deal with other aspects of leadership. For now, notice how each activity or role could contribute to creating a richer spiritual environment in your workplace or community:

- Knowing and speaking about what you think and feel, and being able to articulate clearly a vision for integrating spiritual life and leadership.
- Listening to what others are saying, helping them to clarify their experience, and encouraging them to express their vision for more effective spiritual leadership.
- Observing what you see, hear, think, and feel when others talk about their spiritual life and leadership, and offering insights and raising questions.

Something to Think About

God made the soul of a leader to be intimately connected to him and to be the wellspring from which the leader leads and from which strong, visionary, confident leadership flows. The more our spiritual life and leadership are integrated, the more we truly become spiritual leaders. Our spirituality will become the inspiration and power for our leadership, as well as its defining characteristic. Spiritual leadership is what leaders need to thrive and what others are looking for and need from us. With God's help, this vision can become more of a reality for each one who is called to leadership.

What is your vision for growing spiritually and integrating your spiritual life and leadership?

CONNECTING TO GOD

Leadership Practice
Actively cultivate your own spiritual life.

Soul Principle
Spiritual vitality flows from a real change
of heart and mind toward God.

The spiritual life is above all about the quality of our connection to God. Specific religious observance, moral behavior, and community service often flow from a vital spirituality, but they are not a substitute for something far deeper and more personal. At its core, a vital spiritual life is about a dynamic, loving relationship with God through Jesus Christ, which transforms our thinking, feeling, and acting.

The apostle Paul described the good news of the gospel to the Colossians as "Christ in you, the hope of glory" (Col. 1:28 NIV). The goal of the spiritual life is nothing less than union with Christ that leads to our complete transformation, which comes about through Christ's presence and activity within us, to which we respond in submission and obedience. Thus, Paul explains to the Colossians, "It is he [Christ] whom we proclaim, warning everyone and teaching everyone in all wisdom, so that we may present everyone mature in Christ" (Col. 1:29 NIV). Ultimately, Paul envisions that we will mature spiritually to become more and more like Christ (Rom. 8:29).

Christian philosopher and author Dallas Willard similarly focuses on the power and effect of a relationship with Christ. He describes spiritual vitality as our ability to "follow and become like Jesus . . . with the ease and power he had—flowing from the inner depths, acting with quiet force from the innermost mind and soul of the Christ who has become a real part of us."[1]

However, though we are repeatedly told that our own relationship with God must be our number-one priority, we commonly neglect that relationship. We may not give our spiritual life much thought, or we may fool ourselves into thinking that we can subsist on leftovers from the spiritual highs and enthusiasms of younger days. We may give minimal attention to receiving spiritual enrichment from various sources, or we may make do with the meager diets that the churches we attend offer us.

Those of us who serve as pastors may rarely worship without being preoccupied with the logistics of the service or how it is being received by others. In fact, the demands on our lives, the small margins in our busy schedules, and the energy we spend on our own favorite pastimes don't leave much time or emotional strength for praying, reading, and reflecting on Scripture, or participating regularly in any other spiritual practice.

Perhaps we feel close to God, but we're not really growing in our spiritual life. We have faith, but we feel stuck spiritually. That is, we may trust in Christ for our salvation, but we long for more in our relationship with God and don't know what to do differently. We simply don't see the transformation we had hoped for or that is needed for us to be the spouse, the parent, the leader, the boss, or the brother or sister in Christ that we would like to be. It's not a very satisfying place spiritually, but too often it is where we find ourselves.

All of these realities can add up to spiritual depletion, weariness, frustration, and disappointment with God, our spiritual life, others, and ourselves. We may know the right theology and the ideals of spiritual vitality, but we sometimes feel mired in the sloughs of our daily routine and unsatisfying relationships. What is the way forward? What hope is there for us to experience more of the abundant spiritual life Christ promised?

What's Needed

Actively cultivate your own spiritual life.

For our spiritual life to become the abundant life Christ intends for us, first we need to be committed to seeing things change. Second, we need to recognize that God is taking the initiative to help us develop a more vital spiritual life. Third, we need to find a fresh way to think about our spiritual life and to discover how to connect with God more meaningfully. In short, if we want our relationship with God to improve, we need to cultivate our spiritual life with God's help. We need to work at it, take full advantage of God's reaching out to us, and try new ways of drawing God into every aspect of our life. We need to take responsibility for our relationship to God, just as we would in any relationship that we care about and want to see improved. If we're dissatisfied, we need to do something about it.

However, sometimes when we are told that we need to be more committed to our spiritual life or to go deeper spiritually, the challenge is not helpful. The charge just feels like pressure. It's one more duty on an already overwhelming list of expectations and responsibilities. Sometimes the push comes from external sources, sometimes from within ourselves. Either way, even if a deeper spiritual life is exactly what we are longing for, thinking that it is something we "have to" achieve or experience can make us feel a wide range of negative emotions. We may feel inadequate, frustrated, or sad, because we don't know what to do differently. We may feel like giving up, or we may be just plain mad, because the goal seems unattainable.

Having any of these negative feelings probably means that we are spiritually stuck. We are discouraged because we are not experiencing a vital spiritual life, and either we don't know what to do about it or we don't have the energy to try what we do know. We want to go forward, but either we're spinning our wheels or we've come to a dead standstill—and that probably means that we are going backward.

What went wrong? A prime reason we get stuck spiritually is that we mistakenly think our spiritual growth depends primarily on us. We must remember that we are dependent on the grace of God for spiritual vitality, or there is no going forward. More than that, we are going to feel much better about seeking God when we realize that God is actually taking the initiative to help us grow closer to him.

Thus, I am not at all suggesting that spiritual growth is simply a matter of working harder or longer to become more holy or pleasing to God, though there is certainly a place for discipline and spiritual practices in our lives. Many of us have tried the "gut it out" or "make it happen" approach, and we got worn out. Taking responsibility for our spiritual growth does not mean trying harder on our own. It means giving our conscious attention to what God is doing and wants to do in our life, and then responding accordingly.

The grace of God gives us an opportunity to relate to God in fresh, new ways. We can experience forgiveness and a change of heart that remove the alienation from God we may have felt. God's grace also produces love for God in our hearts through the Holy Spirit. God's grace includes his loving activity in our lives to draw us to him and to lead us into the abundant life. Our part is to respond to God's grace affirmatively and actively, so that we can experience more of what God has in mind for each of us.

To this end, Episcopal priest and author Martin Smith offers a positive approach to prayer and connecting with God that has been transformative for me. Smith suggests that when we become aware of something in our life that doesn't meet God's expectations or our own, we regard the pinpricks of guilt or other negative feelings as a positive sign that God is communicating with us.[2] For example, if we suddenly remember that we haven't spent much time praying or reading Scripture, we may be receiving a loving reminder from God that our life comes from God. The nudge is meant not to condemn or discourage us, but to encourage us to go to God for the support and help we need.

God is not waiting with folded arms for us to initiate contact with him through more frequent quiet times and prayer. God has already initiated communication with us and is simply waiting for our reply. God has chosen to establish a more vital connection to us and to help us grow spiritually. Seeing him as the initiator makes it easier for us to engage in the relationship, just as it is easier for most of us to answer a ringing telephone than to make the effort to call someone we're thinking about.

We pray, then, to carry on the conversation that God is routinely initiating.[3] When we're walking in nature and suddenly feel like giving thanks, God has already been speaking to us in creation, "wooing [us] back from isolation into belonging and from anxiety to life-giving awareness."[4] We are responding to God, not initiating.

When we read the Bible or enjoy a delightful conversation with a friend, and when our thoughts turn to God in praise, remorse, a desire to know more, or intercession for someone, we are responding to God's Spirit gently, or not so gently, calling to us to turn our hearts and minds heavenward.[5]

Redefining prayer in this way, Smith argues, heightens our awareness of God's communication to us and makes us more receptive to the messages we receive. Smith explains further:

> Instead of trying to generate words and feelings to get prayer going, then straining to hear an immediate reply to our opening gambit, paying attention to God's approach comes first. Prayer [then] is primarily attentiveness to God's disclosure to us and the heart's response to that disclosure.[6]

Drawing on Smith's insights, I have learned to say thank you when I am reminded of a failing or lack in my life. I might say silently or aloud, "Thank you, God, for bringing ――― [my need] to my attention and for helping me to remember you and your calling on my life." Or: "Thank you for reminding me that ――― [a sinful attitude or practice] undermines the abundant life Christ intends for me, and that I need to refocus my mind and heart."

Sometimes when I am feeling anxious or overwhelmed with my responsibilities, I suddenly remember, "I should take time to read my Bible. I should take time to pray. I really should make it to worship." I have more to do than I know how to handle, and I'm feeling guilty about neglecting God and my spiritual life. Yet I am not necessarily motivated by these "shoulds." I don't want to add one more thing to my long "to do" list. I just don't have the energy or willpower.

However, when I realize that my awareness of my spiritual emptiness is being initiated by God out of love and concern for me or for others, my response is entirely different. Instead of having to "get my act together," and feeling guilty, ashamed, or inadequate for not doing the right thing, my first response has become thanksgiving. Why? Because I realize that God is actually reaching out to me to help me. I am turning my head toward God in response to God's calling to me. I am answering his loving call, not initiating a call out of obligation.

This shift in how I think about guilt and prayer works. Instead of feeling worse than I already did, I feel encouragement when I think that God cares enough to lead me back toward him. I view the reminder as help, not condemnation. I don't feel that God is burdening me with another obligation, but that he is giving me an opportunity to experience more of the abundant life in Christ. I realize that my heart's desire, to grow closer to God, is in God's heart, too. He is actively helping me to overcome my own limitations, weaknesses, and failures so that a vital spiritual life can become a reality.

To recap to this point, for our spiritual life to become the abundant life Christ intends for us, we need first to be committed to seeing things change. Second, we need to recognize that God is taking the initiative to help us to develop a more vital spiritual life. And now, third, we need to find fresh ways to think about our spiritual life and how to connect with God more meaningfully and experientially.

This third part of actively cultivating our spiritual life calls for strategically setting a new course for our relationship with God. First, we need to ask ourselves some questions. What beliefs, thoughts, and actions will strengthen our sense of connection to God? What will encourage a more nourishing, nurturing, stimulating, and meaningful relationship with God that not only strengthens our own spiritual life, but becomes a deep well of resources from which we can lead more effectively? Our answers will guide us as we develop our spiritual life.

Those who trust in Christ are already permanently connected to God and cannot be separated from God's love.[7] What's too often missing for many of us is a meaningful experience of this connection and a dynamic awareness of relating to God in a personal way. What's needed is a growing awareness of God's presence and activity in our lives, throughout the day, in an increasingly wide range of contexts.

Think for a moment about an important relationship in your life that significantly influences your thinking and feelings. My wife is the person who comes immediately to my mind. The more I love my wife and the more I am aware of her love for me, the more my thinking is affected by our relationship. I may call to mind her words of encouragement or advice as I go through my day. I may pause more often to look at her picture on my desk and smile. I may be more likely to consider how my decisions at work or in my personal life will affect her. I will call to see how her day is going or to share mine—especially if things aren't going so well. I will plan ahead to be sure that I spend regular time with her so that we feel connected, and that we take special trips together to deepen our relationship.

Similarly, the more our love for God grows, the more we will be thinking about and communicating to God naturally, and the more we will be inclined to draw God consciously into our daily life. We will take time regularly to focus our attention on God, so that we may feel more connected. We will consider what God thinks as we work, relate to others, and make our plans. We will want to draw God into our consciousness as much as possible, and will want every aspect of our life to be an extension of our relationship with God.

The degree to which we are not aware of God or desirous of living and leading out of our connection to God, the more we are compartmentalizing our life. We may be harboring thoughts or attitudes that run contrary to a loving, devoted relationship with God—such as arrogance, immorality, defiance, stubbornness, or selfishness. Or, more benignly, we may be unaware of how God fits into the various dimensions of our life. After all, we may wonder, what do taking out the garbage, mowing the lawn, balancing the checkbook, watching a movie, or playing with the kids have to do with spirituality?

In our leadership, we may have similar reasons for keeping God and our spiritual life separate from much of what we do. Often, we are just too busy to slow down enough to connect consciously with God and to draw God into our leadership. Sometimes the reason is plain ignorance—we may have never realized that our relationship with God is relevant to how we run meetings, relate to our administrative assistant and other staff members, conduct performance reviews, or fulfill other aspects of our work. Sometimes our pride creates barriers in our relationship to God—we want to prove our ability to succeed on our own. Sometimes our reason for compartmentalizing is more serious—we're doing something we shouldn't be doing, and thinking about God under such circumstances would be very uncomfortable.

Yet, compartmentalized thinking is a dead end for our spiritual life. We won't get past occasional highs and routine religious behavior. No matter what our role in our organization or the church, we need to learn (or relearn what we may have known as children) to become more aware of God's ways of communicating to us and to converse with God in more meaningful ways in every aspect of our life and leadership.

God may reach out to us through dreams, visions, passions, other people, or simply a quiet inner voice to speak truth we need to hear. Discerning what is from God and what is from our imagination or some other source often requires experience and maturity. Our inexperience, combined with the ambiguous nature of whatever message we think we may be receiving from God, makes discernment challenging. We may need to draw on the wisdom of others, just as Samuel did when he needed Eli to help him to identify the voice of the Lord (1 Sam. 3:1-10). Nevertheless, listening for God's voice is critical to a deepened relationship with God and to our leadership.

When we respond to God's initiative, our conversation with him can be verbal or nonverbal, thought or felt, seen or smelt, sensed or imagined. We may pray aloud or silently. We may paint pictures, write songs, recite Scripture, or help someone in need. We may write out the feelings or thoughts we have, sing them, chant them, or whisper them. There are as many ways to commune with God as there are with everyone else in our life.

Regardless of the way we experience communication with God, a key to spiritual transformation is an ever-deepening sense of connection to God—which is both the means and the result of spiritual growth. We will not be able to measure our relationship, but we will usually know when our connection to God seems more vital to us. Except for the rare "dark night of the soul" that St. John of the Cross describes, during which God does not make his presence known to us, we can usually tell how vital our connection is by the love in our hearts, our hope, our peace, our joy, and the degree to which God seems present in and relevant to our life and leadership.

Actively cultivating our spiritual life by consciously connecting with God provides a great opportunity for us. We can draw more strength and encouragement from the One who loves us and is working in us. By responding eagerly to God's initiatives in our life, we will experience even more grace and help to develop a loving relationship with him and to fulfill our God-given purpose in life.

What's Real

Spiritual vitality flows from a real change
of heart and mind toward God.

The call to cultivate our own spiritual life actively is built upon this soul principle: spiritual vitality flows from a real change of heart and mind toward God. More specifically, a vital spiritual life comes from learning, by God's grace, to love God from our hearts, to submit to God in Christ, and to value the Holy Spirit's activity in daily life and leadership. Our efforts to cultivate our spiritual life cannot be mechanical, done grudgingly from a sense of obligation, or be in any way contrived. Rather, we need to seek a stronger connection to God because we truly value our relationship with God and desire to be transformed according to his will.

First, we need to trust that God, our Creator, desires a loving relationship with his beloved creatures before we can progress in developing a meaningful relationship with God. We need a heart that truly longs for and loves God. We must get beyond distrust or fear of God to value genuinely a personal relationship with God.

I'm not suggesting that we can easily create trust and love, especially if we think that God has hurt us, or if we have never known God in a loving, personal way. If we doubt that God loves us, how can we love God? If we believe that God is untrustworthy, we would be foolish to place our trust in God. Many of us face real challenges to loving and trusting God.

Nevertheless, the truth is, without trust and love we will never develop a vital spiritual life. The more we can let in God's love for us, the more we will love God in return. The more we choose to trust God, even and especially in the midst of suffering, the more we will discover the ways in which God is trustworthy.[8] As our love and trust grow, so will our sense of connection to God become more vibrant and life-giving for us.

Second, in cultivating a vital spiritual life, the fundamental spiritual question for many is one of submission: what does it mean for God to be God and for us to be God's creatures? In other words, vital spirituality requires submitting to God and God's will. It means coming to peace with the fact that we are not God and that the Creator has a right to direct his creation. The apostle Paul explained this concept by drawing an analogy to pottery: the potter has the right to do as he pleases with the clay (Rom. 9:21). Not to accept God's authority over us is to live in rebellion—strong words to be sure, but accurate. Without submission to God, we will continually be trying to set our own course and to establish our own standards of judgment for ourselves (and others), and we will ultimately wind up living for ourselves at the expense of our God-given purpose in life.

Some people resist the role or value of submission in their spiritual life, because they reject any notion that God is distinct from his creation. They may believe that spirituality is about being in harmony with the "God" that is within them— historically known as a form of pantheism (all is God) or panentheism (all is in God, God is in all), rendering the notion of submission to a god nonsensical, irrelevant, unhelpful, or disruptive to their spiritual life. The danger of resisting submission to God is that we may fool ourselves into thinking that we are communing with God, while we are actually worshiping or serving ourselves. Of course, those who think they have submitted to God can fool themselves, too, but that doesn't nullify the basic concern here: without recognizing our need to submit to God, we are bound to set up and serve a rival god in our hearts and minds.

Scripture affirms that human life comes from and perpetually depends on God (for example, see Acts 17:28), and thus in a sense God is connected to all of us. Yet biblical writers call for submitting to or obeying God as an appropriate response to our Creator, who has a personal identity distinct from his creation.[9] Jesus himself was commended for his attitude and response of submission to God the Father (Heb. 5:7).

And what does submission mean? Essentially, submitting to God means giving ourselves wholeheartedly to serving God's purposes in the world. This giving includes developing the relationship with God that he intends for us and living to bring God honor and glory through everything we do. As we glorify God by our faith in Christ and our transformed life of love, others will better see God's true nature of goodness, love, and mercy, and know that salvation is in Jesus Christ.

Paul expressed our call to live to serve God's purposes in several ways. To the Colossians, he said: "And whatever you do, in word or deed, do everything in the name of the Lord Jesus, giving thanks to God the Father through him" (Col. 3:17 NRSV). To the Corinthians, he wrote: "So, whether you eat or drink, or whatever you do, do everything for the glory of God" (1 Cor. 10:31 NRSV). In his second letter to the Corinthians, he said, "For God, who said, 'Let light shine out of darkness,' made his light shine in our hearts to give us the light of the knowledge of the glory of God in the face of Christ. . . . All this is for your benefit, so that the grace that is reaching more and more people may cause thanksgiving to overflow to the glory of God" (2 Cor. 4:6, 15 NIV).

To the Philippians, Paul pointed to Christ as the great example of how to think about ourselves and how to respond to God's will for our life. Though he had a right to declare his divine nature, Christ chose instead to adopt an attitude of humble submission and service to God, which ultimately brings glory to God. Paul said:

> Your attitude should be the same as that of Christ Jesus: Who, being in very nature God, did not consider equality with God something to be grasped, but made himself nothing, taking the very nature of a servant, being made in human likeness. And being found in appearance as a man, he humbled himself and became obedient to death—even death on a cross! Therefore God exalted him to the highest place and gave him the name that is above every name, that at the name of Jesus every knee should bow, in heaven and on earth and under the earth, and every tongue confess that Jesus Christ is Lord, to the glory of God the Father.
>
> Philippians 2:5-11 NIV

Jesus Christ, then, is both the example of submission to God the Father, and the one to whom we submit, because God has made him our Lord (or supreme head and leader). As we bend the "knees" of our hearts and minds to Christ, and acknowledge him as our rightful leader, we bring glory to God.

In broader terms, consultant and author C. Michael Thompson describes spirituality as a right relationship with God based on appropriate attitudes toward God and God's will. Using the "higher power" language reminiscent of the 12 steps of Alcoholic Anonymous and similar recovery groups, Thompson concludes:

> Spirituality, then, is a relationship made possible by our opening to the influence of a higher power, our acknowledgment of that power's rightful place, our conscious alignment with its aims, and our assiduous cultivating of its presence.[10]

Instead of using the word submission, Thompson talks about acknowledgment of God's (the higher power's) "rightful place" and aligning with God's purposes. He also emphasizes here the importance of our "assiduous[ly] cultivating [God's] presence" in our life, which leads us to the third implication of the soul principle related to cultivating our spiritual life: spiritually vital people value the Spirit's activity in their daily life and leadership.

If our relationship with God is characterized by love, trust, and submission, then it follows that we will also value and seek God's presence and activity in every aspect of our life and leadership. Above all, we will let the love we have for God become the controlling influence in every aspect of our life.

Jesus alluded to the pervasive nature of the spiritual life and love when he identified the greatest commandments: "You shall love the Lord your God with all your heart, and with all your soul, and with all your mind, and with all your strength. The second is this, 'You shall love your neighbor as yourself.' There is no other commandment greater than these" (Mark 12:30-31 NRSV).

For Christians, loving God and others is made possible through the presence of the Holy Spirit in our life. The apostle Paul writes, "God's love has been poured into our hearts through the Holy Spirit that has been given to us" (Rom. 5:5 NRSV). The fruit of the Spirit begins with love (Gal. 5:22). Loving others is more important than any other spiritual gift or act of service (1 Cor. 13).

If we love God from our hearts, in our minds, with our souls, and through our actions, being committed to serving God's will above our own, we will see the tremendous importance of doing so in every way possible in our leadership. If we do not serve God from the same depth of love with which we worship God, and by the same Spirit, then our leadership has been compartmentalized—separated from our own personal relationship with God. Whether it is fear, pride, arrogance, ignorance, or some personal agenda, anything that keeps us from consciously connecting with God in our work will stifle our spiritual life and undermine our ability to serve effectively as spiritual leaders.

Spiritual vitality doesn't just happen. For us to be spiritually vital people, we need a real change of heart and mind toward God, which can happen only by regularly seeking a stronger connection with God. We must learn to love and trust God, to submit to God in Christ, and to value the Spirit's activity in our daily life and leadership. The more we see our relationship with God as the great source of nurture, support, and help that it is, the more we will be motivated to connect with God in as many ways as possible, as often as possible, in the midst of work and apart from it.

Here's Help

Practicing the Presence of God

Brother Lawrence championed the spiritual discipline that focuses on living with a continual sense of God—in his words, "practicing the presence of God."[11] Brother Lawrence was not an academic writer or a lofty theologian. He lived in community and had many mundane daily responsibilities as a member of the Carmelite order (Order of Our Lady of Mount Carmel) in 17th-century Paris. Many of his practices refer to ways he connected with God while washing dishes, working in the garden, or doing other commonplace chores.

Simply put, "practicing the presence of God" is not about mountaintop experiences or Damascus-road revelations. It means being aware, attentive, and responsive to God's presence in one's life in every conceivable circumstance.

We know of Brother Lawrence's thoughts and practices from letters and conversations first published in 1692, one year after his death. Since Brother Lawrence did not present his views systematically, I offer my own analysis and synthesis of his enduring contributions to individuals and leaders who are committed to their own spiritual growth and ongoing sense of connection with God.

Motivation and Goals

Brother Lawrence sought to live with a constant awareness of the presence of God above all, out of his appreciation for God's love for him.[12] In addition, he mentioned other important motivations:

- To fulfill God's will rather than seek your own benefit.[13]
- To love and delight yourself in God.[14]
- To feed and nourish your soul with a high notion of God.[15]

Brother Lawrence understood what M. Craig Barnes, former pastor of National Presbyterian Church in Washington, D.C., and now professor of leadership and ministry at Pittsburgh Theological Seminary, describes as the place of our greatest fulfillment—a close relationship with God. God is the "home" we are all seeking, Barnes explains, whether we know it or not.[16] What he means is that all of us were made to love God and to be in relationship with God; that is our primary created purpose. If we seek security, comfort, fulfillment, or peace—that is, "home"—in anything other than our relationship with God, we will be unsatisfied.

Unfortunately, many of us are unaware of our deep longing for God; we know the feelings of emptiness and yearning, but we do not know what is causing them or what to do about them. Even pastors and other professional ministers, in spite of regularly preaching, teaching, or counseling, may no longer be (or may never have been) in touch with their true heart's desire for God.

For those who have lost touch with their love for God, the first step in cultivating their spiritual life and relationship with God is to pray to be able to see or experience God's love and to be able to love God in return. Without God's love for us and our love for God, all attempts to grow spiritually will be hollow and misguided.

Methods and Practices

Our dependence on a loving relationship with God for spiritual vitality makes it important to guard our hearts from anything that dulls or steals our hunger, thirst, and love for God. Even more, connecting with God usually necessitates that we actively nurture our longing and love for God, which involves specific spiritual practices. Though our spiritual life depends on the grace of God, there is no substitute for our active response to God's working in our life. Brother Lawrence identified many actions that are important in cultivating one's sense of connection to God:

- Trust in God in every possible way.[17]
- Renounce everything that doesn't lead to God.[18]
- Recognize and experience God as intimately present.[19]
- Pray for a sense of the presence and love of God.[20]
- Worship as often as possible.[21]
- Recall God's holy presence when you have forgotten.[22]
- Drive away distracting thoughts.[23]
- Give simple attention and general fond regard to God; that is, carry on a habitual, silent, and secret conversa-

tion with God from your soul.[24]

- Always work at being aware of God; be devoted and determined.[25]
- Think of God that you may know God that you may love God.[26]
- Pray for an ability to endure suffering with courage, and for faith to see God's work in your suffering for good.[27]

Brother Lawrence saw focusing on God as the number-one priority of his life. While it did not take him away from his work and community life, his relationship with God was pre-eminent in his thinking in the midst of all else he did. His practices suggest that those who want to deepen their connection to God need to make some decisions. Some are big, some are small; some relate to attitudes, some to priorities; some to weekly schedule, some to daily practices. Yet at the core, all of the choices come down to two key decisions: Will we trust? Will we act?

Application: The Four Ways

In practice, Brother Lawrence's various methods may be synthesized as four ways he quietly looked for and observed God's presence in him and around him. Gerald May introduced his thoughtful interpretation of these four ways to me at the Shalem Institute, and he discusses them in detail in his book *The Awakened Heart.*[28] The following draws heavily on May's synthesis of Brother Lawrence's practices, in ascending order of awareness and intention.

Way 1: Brief awareness of God. The simplest and lightest of ways to become more conscious of God's presence is prompted by a sudden, often brief, awareness of God. Something happens inside us in response to some stimulus, known or unknown, which brings to mind God's presence and activity in our lives. Gerald May calls such an experience a "little instant of remembering love after we have been forgetful." Our experience becomes:

The reminding, the remembering, the wonderful returning to love's present moment. [Brother Lawrence] called it the little interior glance. The interior glance does not necessarily mean looking inward; it simply *happens* interiorly. It is a contemplative look Godward. It is an attitude of the heart leaning toward the truth of God's presence, or a flash of the mind opening to the remembrance of being in love. . . . Little interior glances are simple things: unadorned remembrances and noticings happening within the ordinary activities of our daily lives. They come and go. They are not to be held on to.[29]

For example, a passing chill in the spine—tingles—may be a physiological response to a sudden awareness of God. An "aha" experience, in which we suddenly sense that God might be at work in something or someone, connects us to God mentally and emotionally. Perceiving a turn of events as a little gift of kindness from God or suddenly being able to see humor in trying circumstances may awaken our sense of connection and strengthen our faith.

These examples illustrate that this first way is in fact *not* something we create or initiate. Brief awareness of God comes from something God does in us as an act of grace, in the midst of our daily lives. We simply pause long enough to take notice.

We can increase our awareness of God by finding ways to help us to remember God and to recall how God works in our lives. We can read Scripture to refresh our memories as to the character of God, which includes loving mercy that is renewed every morning (e.g., Lam. 3:19-26). One of the most valuable benefits of participating in worship, meditation, fellowship, and other spiritual practices is that they help us to remember what God has done, what we might expect from God, and what we might hope for.

Often the best place to begin deepening our spiritual life is to ask God for help to do what we believe God is calling us to do. Brother Lawrence says, "Pray for a sense of the presence and love of God."[30] Pray for God to help you to see what you need to see and to remember what you need to remember to be refreshed, encouraged, and full of faith.

While the skeptic might dismiss any ambiguous experience as the product of chance or chemistry, the believer remains open to however God might be touching his or her life in a brief instance in the course of a day. As leaders, we will not only draw strength personally from the little interior glances that we experience, but we can also strengthen our leadership by encouraging others to do the same. We cultivate a more vibrant spiritual atmosphere in the workplace by promoting greater spiritual awareness among team members or others whom we are leading. We are functioning as spiritual leaders.

Way 2: A simple heart prayer. The prayer of the heart is Brother Lawrence's second way of practicing the presence of God.[31] Heart prayers continue more or less all the time within us, though they may be expressed aloud at times. A short phrase, a particular word, or a favorite name for God, which we recite to symbolize our desire for God, may be used. As noted earlier, Brother Lawrence calls this practice "giv[ing] simple attention and general fond regard to God; . . . carry[ing] on an habitual, silent, and secret conversation with God from your soul."[32]

Heart prayers can be calls for help from God, appeals for reassurance or comfort, requests for mercy and grace, or anything that comes from our heart that reaches out to connect with God in some way. For example, various biblical prayers were eventually blended together over the centuries to create one of the best-known and most frequently used heart prayers among Christians: "Lord Jesus Christ, Son of God, have mercy upon me, a sinner."[33]

When I feel overwhelmed or anxious, sometimes I simply call out the name "Jesus." I may not have the words or the energy to say anything more, but I want to connect. I need help. Saying Jesus' name is not a magical incantation, but it brings me comfort and helps me to feel more linked to God.

Brother Lawrence recommends that ministers preach the practice of the presence of God above all other things, and that spiritual directors do the same. Nothing is sweeter or more delightful, he says, than a continual conversation with God. The more we understand and experience the grace and assistance of God that is available to us, the more we will do everything within our power to keep sight of God and make a "firm resolution" never to forget God. He urges his reader to "set heartily about this work, and if you do it as you ought be assured that you will soon find the effects of it."[34]

Way 3: Live and work in the company of God. Brother Lawrence indicates that we may raise our conscious awareness of God even further by experiencing God in the midst of everything we do. Again, we are not creating a connection to God, but tapping into or becoming more aware of God's presence and activity in our life. May describes the human component of this practice as "living, as best we can, in appreciation of and fidelity to the continual heart-to-heart connectedness with the holy Other whose presence makes us complete."[35]

In addition to trusting that God is present with us, we may seek to live and work in the company of God by using our imagination to visualize his presence. For example, we may envision God sitting next to our daughter (or ourselves) after she has stormed out of the room, slamming the door on the way out. We may imagine Jesus standing next to us in the laundry room or kitchen, when we feel alone or desire a sense of connection. Conceiving of Jesus' actual presence may comfort us in our distress or encourage us to stay the course. We can be at peace, knowing that we are loved, in an enduring relationship with our God, who is present with us—regardless of what happens next.

There are many opportunities for becoming more aware of the presence of God in our daily life and work. For example, we can consciously seek connection with God in a meeting; at dinner with the family or a friend; and when exercising, driving, working at our desk, or counseling. Sometimes I imagine Jesus' presence in the room when I'm meeting with other people. I let my heart, mind, and body shift naturally in any way that flows from becoming more conscious of his presence. At times I have found myself sitting up straighter; sometimes I start taking the other person more seriously; at other times I have felt myself becoming more humble or more caring in my thoughts. The quality of my communication improves, and often it seems that my ability to be used by God constructively in that situation increases.

One word of caution, however. Be sure to conceive of God's presence in positive terms, unlike the frightening image some of us received as children. One Sunday school song I remember went something like this:

Oh be careful, little eyes, what you see,
Oh, be careful, little eyes, what you see;
For the Father up above
Is looking down in love,
So be careful, little eyes, what you see.

Subsequent stanzas warn to "be careful, litle ears, what you hear"; "be careful, little tongue, what you say"; "be careful, little hands, what you do"; and "be careful, little feet, where you go." Talk about a mixed message! God in heaven is looking at us with love, but watch out. He's going to get us if we step out of line.

An awareness of God's presence is not supposed to terrify us, but to improve the quality of our spiritual life and our ability to love others. To live and work in the company of God means carrying the sense of awareness of God with us as we relate to others and perform our daily duties. The goal is to draw strength, encouragement, perspective, love, and whatever else God has to offer into our lives in a more conscious way, so that we may experience God more fully and may reflect God to others more meaningfully. Brother Lawrence was particularly known for experiencing and reflecting God.

His very countenance was edifying; such a sweet and calm devotion appearing in it as could not but affect the beholders.

And it was observed that in the greatest hurry of business in the kitchen he still preserved his recollection and heavenly-mindedness . . . with an even uninterrupted composure and tranquility of spirit. "The time of business," said he, "does not with me differ from the time of prayer; and in the noise and clutter of my kitchen, while several persons are at the same time calling for different things, I possess God in as great tranquility as if I were upon my knees at the Blessed Sacrament."[36]

I am still waiting for the day when someone might easily describe me as a tranquil person with an edifying countenance, but I *have* seen the difference it makes to seek to serve and to lead with a greater awareness of God's presence in the moment. Though far from perfect, I have become less reactive to or harsh with others and more conscious of trying to communicate God's love to staff members and co-workers. I am seeing an improvement in the quality of my counseling and conflict-resolution skills. I am quicker to apologize if I have overreacted to someone, and more eager to forgive.

Brother Lawrence offers us not simply an ideal, but a picture we may envision and a practice we may emulate. His perspective and example offer us hope as individuals, and, as we begin to experience God's presence more and more in the midst of our leadership, they also offer hope to everyone who has to work with us!

Way 4: Contemplation. Brother Lawrence's fourth way extends Way 3. We are not only aware of God in daily life, but we also focus on God in increasingly deep and profound ways. Brother Lawrence instructs us to "think of God that you may know God that you may love God."[37] This is the goal and way of contemplation.

In summing up the meaning and value of contemplation, May concludes that "what God wants, and what our hearts most deeply seek, is for us to live every moment, do every act, breathe every breath in conscious immediacy with the One who is all love."[38] Simply put, contemplation is opening ourselves to God to see and experience God in greater and greater fullness.

Contemplation, though it is the fruit of God's initiative in our life, is often experienced as a result of the intentional focusing of our minds on God, which is simply prayer. Martin Smith explains that the source and the focus of contemplative prayer is God, in all three persons. The Holy Spirit prompts prayer by "actively engaging the depths of our heart and stirring us from within."[39] In what Smith calls meditative prayer that leads to contemplation, we gaze on Christ.[40] Our goal will be to come "to 'know the love of Christ which surpasses knowledge.' In prayer we expose ourselves to God's love in Christ, and allow ourselves to experience it."[41] Ultimately, though, "we find ourselves turned with [Christ] in the direction in which he gazes, that is into the face of the utter mystery of God which can never be pinned down or captured . . . [that we might become] unrestrainedly in love with God."[42]

Contemplation can take place in a wide variety of settings and as part of numerous spiritual disciplines. It usually involves relaxation, stillness, and focus.[43] One of my favorite places to contemplate God is sitting in front of a crucifix. One can contemplate just about anywhere, but I like the quietness of a church and the figure of Jesus to help me to stay focused. I sit there in silence. I heed Brother Lawrence's instruction to "drive away distracting thoughts,"[44] by simply letting them cross my mind and refusing to engage them. I focus on Jesus on the cross without any prescribed thoughts or ideas. I remain open to whatever God may want to bring to my attention or to reveal to me. Sometimes, I receive thoughts about specific situations or gain new insight. At other times, there is only silence. Either way, I often leave feeling at peace and renewed.

Each of us needs to find our own ways to practice the presence of God. I recommend establishing a solid connection to God at the beginning of each day by reading Scripture, praying, and brief journal writing. Then, develop habits of prayer and Brother Lawrence's practices throughout the day.[45] The next chapter offers many suggestions for methods of developing other spiritual disciplines.

Something to Think About

One of the greatest aids to my daily spiritual life and ability to connect to God mentally and emotionally has been journal writing. All you need is a blank piece of paper and a pen or, my favorite, a laptop computer. Journaling is a great way to know and examine what you are thinking and feeling, and to express in a confidential manner what you most want to say. The more we know what is going on inside us, the less power negative emotions have, and the more power we can give to those beliefs and values that we cherish. Often, my writing has helped me to see problems in my thinking or to uncover some deep pain or concern. Journal writing often leads me also to prayer. Once I know what I am thinking and feeling, my prayers often flow more naturally and meaningfully.

In this chapter we've been focusing on connecting with God and committing ourselves to developing our spiritual life. Here are some questions to think about. Try writing out your answers in a journal, or use the space provided below. Then, consider using these questions as a guide for reflection and discussion with co-workers or others who seek to serve more effectively as spiritual leaders. Ask yourself:

- How welcome is God as my constant companion and co-worker?

- How do I seek to connect with God throughout my day?

- What works best? What isn't working well?

- What is something I want to do differently to help me to better connect with God in the midst of my life and work?

SPIRITUAL 3 DISCIPLINES

Leadership Practice
Develop specific spiritual disciplines.

Soul Principle
Disciplines deepen our spiritual life
and empower our leadership.

I hate discipline.

Now, I like the idea of being a disciplined person. I usually feel good when I act in a disciplined manner. I certainly see the tremendous benefit of being disciplined.

It's the act of having to be disciplined that I find so unappealing. It's not being able to do what I *feel* like doing at any given moment that seems so hard at times. Even with the best of intentions, I sometimes find myself running out of steam or getting distracted more often than I would like.

Nonetheless, to the extent that I have practiced them, spiritual disciplines have been transformative in my life and leadership. They have helped me to move from good intentions and vague aspirations to real experience with God and meaningful transformation. They also have changed the way that I relate to co-workers and approach issues and difficulties, because they change me, and my leadership can't help but be affected.

As leaders, we need disciplines to deepen us and to strengthen both our commitment and our ability to offer spiritual leadership through the daily challenges we face. In this chapter, I offer some of the spiritual tools that have been particularly helpful to me, and that have been practiced by some of the most respected spiritual leaders in the history of Christianity.

What's Needed

Develop specific spiritual disciplines.

To address the need for Christians to deepen their spiritual life, certain practices, known as spiritual disciplines, have been developed over the centuries. One of the best-known teachers who has brought these practices into the mainstream of Christianity, Richard Foster, divides the classic disciplines into three categories: inward, outward, and corporate. The inward disciplines are meditation, prayer, fasting, and study. The outward disciplines are simplicity, solitude, submission, and service. The corporate ones are confession, worship, guidance, and celebration.[1]

Practicing spiritual disciplines cultivates a conscious sense of the presence and activity of God in our life through intention and consistency. The goal is to produce concrete change in our attitudes and behaviors that will, in turn, increase our effectiveness in all spheres of our life, including leadership.

Dallas Willard, in his thoughtful and challenging book *The Spirit of the Disciplines: Understanding How God Changes Lives,* rightly explains the role of disciplines in terms of our cooperation with God:

The disciplines are activities of mind and body purposefully undertaken, to bring our personality and total being into effective cooperation with the divine order. They enable us more and more to live in a power that is, strictly speaking, beyond us, deriving from the spiritual realm itself, as we "yield ourselves to God, as those that are alive from the dead, and our members as instruments of righteousness unto God," as Romans 6:13 puts it.[2]

Spiritual disciplines are not magical. They are tools that God uses to release us from the power of our sinful impulses and to help us come alive to what the Holy Spirit is doing in our lives. When done with a right understanding of their purpose and value, they can bring us closer to God and make us better prepared to serve God daily. However, we need to actually do them to grasp their significance and to benefit from them.

What's Real

Spiritual disciplines deepen our spiritual life
and empower our leadership.

Many New Testament passages indicate that God's work in us, through Christ and the Holy Spirit, is the means by which we are transformed.[3] At the same time, each epistle includes exhortations and practical instructions to live worthily of the gospel (Phil. 1:27), to please God (1 Thess. 4:1), and to live out the Christian life appropriately.[4] It's not always clear, though, what the relationship is between God's part and our part in our transformation.

In Peter's second epistle we find helpful insight into this perplexing issue. He resolves the tension between who is responsible for our transformation—God or us—by answering "both." We are changed as we consciously draw upon God's power within us. He explains:

[God's] divine power has given us everything we need for life and godliness through our knowledge of him who called us by his own glory and goodness. Through these he has given us his very great and precious promises, so that through them you may participate in the divine nature and escape the corruption in the world caused by evil desires.

2 Peter 1:3-4 NIV

Our source of power comes from our participating in the "divine nature" available to believers through the Holy Spirit. Peter is not saying that believers become God or gods, but that the power of God is at work in the life of Christians to enable them to break free from the corrupting influence of evil. Our part is to draw on God's power to move in a positive direction away from sin by incorporating the attributes and values of God into our life, as the following verses suggest.[5]

For this very reason, you must make every effort to support your faith with goodness, and goodness with knowledge, and knowledge with self-control, and self-control with endurance, and endurance with godliness, and godliness with mutual affection, and mutual affection with love.

2 Peter 1:5-7 NRSV

Real change takes place in our lives as we make a conscious attempt to adopt the qualities that fit God's will for every Christian, many of which are listed in the verses cited above. Paul creates a helpful metaphor to explain the concept when he urges believers to think about personal transformation in terms of changing our clothing. He writes to the Ephesians:

For surely you have heard about [Christ] and were taught in him, as truth is in Jesus. You were taught to put away your former way of life, your old self, corrupt and deluded by its lusts, and to be renewed in the spirit of your minds, and to clothe yourselves with the new self, created according to the likeness of God in true righteousness and holiness.

Ephesians 4:21-24 NRSV

Paul, then, provides the Ephesians a host of examples of what it means to put off the old self, be renewed in the spirit of our minds, and put on the new self. The attributes we find in Peter's and Paul's writings are not spiritual disciplines per se, but they are the fruit of a vital connection to God. They flow from our making use of God's power within us, which the disciplines strengthen.

As we pursue the transformation God makes possible, we will grow spiritually and become more fruitful in our lives. If we don't seek to grow spiritually, we will miss out on much of what God intends for us. Peter expresses this reality in stark terms:

> For if you possess these qualities in increasing measure, they will keep you from being ineffective and unproductive in your knowledge of our Lord Jesus Christ. But if anyone does not have them, he is nearsighted and blind, and has forgotten that he has been cleansed from his past sins.
>
> 2 Peter 1:8-9 NIV

Peter implies that it is possible for someone to receive the grace of God for forgiveness and yet not be transformed as God intends. That is, we can be "cleansed from past sins" but not go on to experience the personal development that belongs to the Christian life—the goodness, knowledge, self-control, perseverance, godliness, brotherly kindness, and love that Peter writes about. But that need not be our fate.

Transformation is possible for everyone; but a commitment to action on the part of the believer is needed. Peter expresses what's needed and the benefits of making the effort to develop our spiritual life this way:

> Therefore, brothers and sisters, be all the more eager to confirm your call and election, for if you do this, you will never stumble. For in this way, entry into the eternal kingdom of our Lord and Savior Jesus Christ will be richly provided for you.
>
> 2 Peter 1:10-11 NRSV

Setting spiritual goals for our lives, drawing on God's power within us, and making "every effort" to adopt godly characteristics are all important ingredients of spiritual growth. Peter teaches that such behavior will affirm our identity as God's children and keep us from falling into sin. Our transformation will also greatly enhance our experience of entering into heaven. Peter doesn't explain what he means by the latter benefit of transformation, which the New International Version expresses as a "rich welcome," but we can imagine that God will express his joy over our spiritual growth when we arrive in his presence. In any case, Peter's main point is that we have a lot to do with our spiritual growth and personal transformation, and that great benefits accrue from making the effort to grow.

Does this sound like heresy? It's not. Paul also calls believers to make an effort to develop their character and godliness (i.e., godlike qualities) with the help of God. For example, in his letter to the Philippians, he says, "Work out your salvation with fear and trembling; for it is God who is at work in you, enabling you both to will and to work for his good pleasure" (Phil. 2:12-13). Thus, while God's grace and power at work within us are necessary for us to experience the abundant life Christ envisions for us, developing this life requires our active response to God's work within us.[6]

In other words, we have a critical role to play in our spiritual life. Neither Peter nor Paul suggests in any way that Christians need to earn their salvation. They are saying that the transformed life, characterized by such qualities as greater integrity, love, obedience, vitality, and effectiveness in service, are the result of our concerted effort, enabled by the grace and power of God.

Dallas Willard makes this same point unequivocally:

> Spiritual growth and vitality stem from what we actually *do* with our lives, from the *habits* we form, and from the *character* that results. True character transformation begins, we are taught to believe, in the pure grace of God and is continually assisted by it. Very well. But *action* is also indispensable in making the Christian truly a different kind of person—one having a new life in which, as 2 Corinthians 5:17

states, "Old things have passed away and, behold, all things become new." Failure to act in certain definite ways will guarantee that this transformation does not come to pass.[7]

Willard is arguing that we need to practice spiritual disciplines so that we can develop healthful life habits that produce character, which in turn creates spiritual growth and vitality. He's right to draw a connection between our life habits and the quality of our spiritual life, yet we should not think that this spiritual development is linear. The process is more like a spiral. God awakens us spiritually by his grace, which motivates us to seek him by practicing spiritual disciplines and developing healthy life habits (e.g., praying regularly, observing the Sabbath, seeking renewal experiences, and engaging in other sound practices). Then, the more we experience God's presence and activity in our life through the disciplines, the more we are motivated to seek him. The spiral continues by alternating and blending our experience of God and our efforts to seek God. All the while, transformation is taking place within us. Depending on how we think of the spiritual life metaphorically, we can imagine the spiral either moving upward to lead us to greater spiritual heights, or moving downward to make us spiritually deeper.

God uses spiritual disciplines to produce the life and leadership he intends for us. The human part of the equation is to practice the disciplines and to seek the godly qualities Peter outlines; the divine part is to give us the desire and power to act, and to produce the inner change God envisions for us. Richard Foster explains this relationship between God's activity and ours well:

> God has given us the Disciplines of the spiritual life as a means of receiving His grace. The Disciplines allow us to place ourselves before God so that He can transform us. . . . We must always remember that the path [i.e., the Disciplines] does not produce the change; it only puts us in the place where the change can occur. This is the way of disciplined grace.[8]

Each discipline connects us to God in a different way and results in our being changed over time. We may desire instant results, but spiritual disciplines are not about quick fixes. They are about reordering our way of life, so that we are continually brought into better connection to God. There the Spirit of God may teach, reshape, nurture, encourage, discipline, empower, and equip us in a wide variety of ways. Thus, spiritual disciplines—or more precisely, God's working through our practice of the disciplines—deepen our spiritual life and empower our leadership.

Here's Help

Despite my occasional resistance to discipline and the inconsistency in my devotional life, I have developed some spiritual practices that have been significant in my own spiritual life and leadership. On the basis of the literature and my own experience, I can wholeheartedly make a number of recommendations.

One good starting place is to read (or reread) Richard Foster's *Celebration of Discipline,* which is still the contemporary classic guide to specific spiritual disciplines.[9] Some excellent recent publications provide a contemporary approach to ancient practices, such as *lectio divina* (holy reading of Scripture) and labyrinth walking.[10] Then, experiment with each discipline, at least three times, to see if you are ready to derive benefit from practicing it. Though the real fruit of most disciplines comes from years of practice, a little taste of a new practice may be a catalyst to continued action.

The following collection of practices and disciplines comes from my own experience. Each one has contributed significantly to my own spiritual life and leadership.

Bible Reading, Journaling, and Prayer

On a daily basis, there is no substitute for the often commended combination of Bible reading, journaling, and prayer. Since I do a lot of biblical teaching, I am naturally drawn to the text from a teacher's point of view. To let God speak to me personally, as well as to gain better and fresh understanding for my teaching, I have adopted a multiple-step process for my daily Bible study. From my experience, I suggest:

- Read the text, pausing on each verse. Then, read the passage as a whole a second time.
- Write down a paraphrase of the main points or key features of the reading.
- In a paragraph labeled "commentary," reflect on the meaning and significance of the text, with an eye toward what you might emphasize if you were to teach on it.
- Then, start a new paragraph, with your initials in all capitals. I write "TCG," followed by whatever strikes me as personally relevant, including what I sense God might be saying to me from the Bible passage. Personal application is essential for spiritual growth through daily Bible reading.
- Conclude with a written prayer expressing your feelings or response to what you have thought about or experienced in your reading.

Daily journal writing does not have to be tied to one's Bible study. In fact, I keep a separate journal (actually, a document on my computer) for my personal life. Writing down my thoughts, feelings, and experiences has been a great way for me to gain insight into myself. For example, I have discovered patterns in my life. I may think that I have received a new insight or that I am encountering a new doubt or new struggle, only to discover that I wrote about that same topic six months or a year before. Journal writing is also cathartic and helpful for working through issues with God. You can be your own sounding board, too, having a dialogue with the person, other than God, who knows and cares about you best—you!

As a discipline, conclude every morning session of Bible reading and journaling with prayer. You can write the prayer in your journal, as recommended above, or speak it aloud.

The point is to respond directly to God with whatever you may have received in your Bible reading and journaling.

Your daily discipline of prayer can also include praying at every mealtime and before going to bed. The Muslim practice of praying five times each day and the Catholic monastic practice of praying seven times daily inspired me to make regular times of prayer for myself and my family. I see the prayers not as obligations, however, but as opportunities to focus my heart and mind on God, on what I am thankful for, and on how God has called me to prioritize my thinking and living.

At bedtime, I pray separately with each child and later with my spouse, except on the days when I'm too tired or drained. Then, I ask someone else to offer the prayer, or we engage in group prayer. The discipline breaks down when I give in to my weariness and don't initiate the prayers at all.

The regular prayers that punctuate your day can be brief, or even formulaic (for example, "Bless this food to our use..."; "Please help us to experience your love and activity in our lives during the day and bring us back together safely tonight; or "Help us to sleep well and to wake rested in the morning, better prepared to serve you"). Yet the richest prayer experiences are usually spontaneous, heartfelt expressions of gratitude or intercession for others in need. As I discussed extensively in the previous chapter, we can also pray informally throughout the day in a wide variety of circumstances as part of practicing the presence of God. Christians have practiced many forms of prayer over the centuries. Explore various ways of connecting with God to find the forms and manners that are most meaningful to you.

Lectio Divina

We can also develop a discipline for reading Scripture, meditating, and praying by regularly joining with other Christians to do so. I participate in a Thursday morning *lectio divina* group. This centuries-old practice is not yet well known among most Christians but addresses the felt need of many in our fast-paced, sound-byte-enamored, frazzled culture. The practice includes up to four readings of the same biblical text, and allows for silence to reflect and pray. It provides a time for quiet, prayerful, and focused attention on whatever theme emerges for the individual as the passage is read and reread. (See appendix A for a common format for a 30–60 minute group *lectio divina* session.) With their use of listening, imagination, application, and meditation—including 20 minutes of complete silence—*lectio divina* sessions often leave me refreshed, better focused, more peaceful, more closely connected to God, and eager to return to leadership.[11]

Christian Fellowship

Devoting time to in-depth, personal relationships is natural for some people, but not for everyone. If we tend to forget about others in our preoccupation with tasks or other activities that are not inherently relational, we may need to create a discipline of participating in Christian fellowship. In addition to helping to meet our social needs, Christian fellowship allows us to share our spiritual journey with friends and others. I am not talking about eating doughnuts in fellowship hall between the services, playing basketball at the gym, or watching the Super Bowl with our Sunday school class, all of which we may enjoy doing. I'm referring to joining in solid, substantive Christian fellowship with one or more individuals that includes talking honestly about how God is at work in our lives, where we are struggling, what we are thankful for, and where we need help.

By way of example, I've been committed to meeting once or twice a month with one of my best friends for mutual encouragement. Over the past 10 years, we have supported and counseled each other as we've wrestled with our own faith, our calling, our marriages, our child-rearing, and other important aspects of our life. We meet for an hour over breakfast, and arrive with no set agenda, except to talk about what's happening in our lives. We split the time evenly, though we don't keep time. We listen carefully to each other, and respond in whatever ways are most appreciated and deemed helpful by the other person. I often leave our times together feeling re-energized, having been supported, challenged, helped, or advised. I also feel joy knowing that I have been helpful to my friend.

Several years ago, to meet different fellowship needs, I formed a small men's group. We meet periodically to talk about how we think God wants us to live our lives in light of our resources and stages of life. The group members shared a felt need to work through similar issues. We intentionally organize our times together so that we won't waste the opportunity. Each guy comes with his own questions or issues for discussion, and I often bring some outside materials or a Bible passage to stimulate conversation. Apart from giving me three good friends, the biggest value of this group for me is to have others to talk to who truly understand the concerns and issues I am facing. I am often challenged to think in new ways, and God uses the others to open my eyes to blind areas in my heart, mind, and life.

Spiritual Direction

I meet monthly with a spiritual director who offers a listening ear and helpful suggestions for cultivating my spiritual life. Once reserved for a small segment of the Christian world, Roman Catholic clergy and devoted laypeople, spiritual direction has increasingly become a great resource to Christians from many traditions. In my experience, the director does very little actual "directing." His work is more a matter of redirecting—helping me to refocus on God. My director routinely asks me what God is doing in my life. Then, when I am floundering in confusion or distress, he gently inquires what God is saying to me about or through the situation at hand. Through spiritual direction, I have been learning to seek God in the midst of my struggles as well as to recognize better how God may be at work in my life all the time.

Spiritual directors offer something that most friends cannot, in a defined, one-way relationship. The spiritual director, a specially trained and mature Christian, enters into a relationship with another person solely for that person's benefit.

Finding a spiritual director may be challenging. I found mine by word of mouth. You could ask local clergy, retreat centers, or seminaries for leads. I recommend a one-hour meeting with a spiritual director once a month in which you will do most of the talking, but with the goal of listening to yourself and to what God may be saying to you through the director and the experience. Payment is usually modest, less than an hour with a therapist, as a rule.

Annual Spiritual Retreat

Once a year, take a week away for a spiritual retreat, focusing the time on rest, renewal, and connection to God. If you cannot afford the vacation time because of family or other commitments, and if your work does not provide time for spiritual revitalization, then you may need to settle for a long weekend at a local retreat center or other suitable spot. The important dimension to this discipline is concentrated time away from normal life and relationships to nurture your spiritual life.

For the past seven years, I've been able to take a full week for a spiritual retreat annually. I've spent my time in a diversity of retreat sites, depending on suggestions from others, finances, and opportunity. I've gone to Taizé, France, to worship with the Christian community there. A few times I've spent a week alone at our family cabin—an option that kept the cost down but still gave me the solitude I desired. One year, I learned meditation in Puerto Vallarta, Mexico (no, not on the beach!), and twice I spent a week at Bon Secours retreat center in Maryland. My favorite place to go is Chartres, France, where a 12th-century cathedral provides a powerful setting for worship, reflection, and prayer. But choosing the location is far less important than blocking out a significant amount of time devoted to connecting with God in a wide variety of ways. A retreat can be done well anywhere that is away from the cell phone, e-mail, TV, videos, the office, and the other trappings of normal life.

During my various retreats I've fasted, hiked, journaled, read, studied, prayed, caught up on sleep, worshiped, kept silence, stayed alone all week, or participated in a group experience. The key is to minimize the distractions and habitual behaviors that tend to fill up our lives or drain our energy, so that we can be quiet long enough to think new thoughts, to hear God speak, to experience the Holy Spirit, to reflect on who Christ is, and to be changed.

To develop this spiritual discipline in your life, you will likely need to find your own way, because chances are, no one is going to take you by the hand to make this happen for you. To get started, pray. Ask God to open your heart and mind to an extended time away with a spiritual focus. Ask for an open door—a suggestion for a place to go, a group to join, an opportunity that would fit your sense of yearning and God's calling. Do some exploring of possible locations by talking to pastors, contacting retreat centers, checking the Web. Make time in your schedule well ahead of time, and stick to it, just as you would any other important appointment. You may want to begin with a weekend away at a local monastery or retreat center, perhaps as a silent retreat or one guided by a spiritual director. A full week away is even better. Ask your employer to consider giving you an additional week as part of your compensation package for the specific purpose of spiritual renewal, or else do it as part of continuing education, or even vacation if need be. Use your imagination, and create something brand new.

Whatever you do, get started. Begin moving in the direction of extended time away with God.

Periodic Spiritual Activities

Periodic spiritual events and select continuing-education opportunities can be quite meaningful, too. Men's or women's retreats, Promise Keepers, labyrinth walks, leadership summits, special events at church, Bible studies, enrichment weekends, and a host of other special events are available to most of us and can help us to grow spiritually. We would not consider them spiritual disciplines per se, because of their unique or infrequent nature, but they can be transformational experiences that set the stage for other spiritual practices.

One particular course has been especially powerful in my personal life and leadership. In 2002, I completed an 18-month program run by the Shalem Institute called "The Soul of the Executive." It included two week-long retreats, special readings, exposure to various spiritual practices, and an extended project designed to help participants offer spiritual leadership in their executive roles. Many of the readings, experiences, and ideas from this course have greatly influenced my own development as a spiritual leader, my teaching on leadership, and the writing of this book.

You will have to find your own way to incorporate spiritual disciplines into your life. The goal is not to follow someone else's spiritual practices or to create an oppressive system of "have-tos." Disciplines are intended to help us to establish sound practices that set us free from some of our compulsions and preoccupations; to create healthy habits; and to foster a more vital and fruitful connection to God. Spiritual disciplines ground us in God that we may have increased ability to live the life that God wants for us and that we most desire.

Something to Think About

What is God saying to you right now?

One helpful spiritual practice is to build enough margin into your life that when you sense God may be speaking to you, you can stop to capture the experience or thoughts in writing, or in a picture, or in some other physical way.

Take a moment to reflect. Record your thoughts in your journal or in the spaces provided below. In light of what you have just read on spiritual disciplines, what might God be communicating to you *right now*? Ask yourself:

- Is there a spiritual practice that God might be calling me to undertake? (If you don't know, do as my spiritual director suggests: enter into a prayerful dialogue with Jesus, as blind Bartimaeus did. First, ask Jesus for help. Wait for a moment, and, in your mind, hear Jesus ask

you what you want. Then express whatever seems most
true about your need in response to his question [Mark
10:46-52]. See if a particular spiritual discipline might
emerge as right for you in light of this conversation with
Christ.)

- What are some concrete steps I will need to take to pursue that one thing that is emerging?

- What obstacles or challenges need to be overcome (e.g.,
  lack of time, others' demands, bad habits, distracting
  routines, need for resources, low energy)?

- What do I sense God is leading me to do next?

Getting Started

Start small—try one thing for one week. Step outside of your box—try one new thing this year. Get help and support—find a kindred spirit, a spiritual director, a fellow pastor, or a spiritually minded friend. Ask God for help—ask God to open your heart, open the way, and provide the resources needed.

When someone first suggested a week-long spiritual retreat, or joining a *lectio divina* group, or starting up spiritual direction, or fasting, or a silent weekend, or any other spiritual practice that was outside of my experience, I usually had the same reaction: "No way! It's not for me. I don't have time. I don't know what to expect (read: 'I'm terrified!'); my plate is already overfilled." And so forth. I couldn't imagine how I could fit them into my life and schedule.

Today, I can't imagine *not* doing them.

ALIGNING
WITH GOD'S PURPOSES

Leadership Practice
Always seek to serve God's purposes first.

Soul Principle
Aligning our will with God's is an all-encompassing,
ongoing process.

What is God's purpose for your life?

We live in a society that glories in the status and accomplishments of human beings, revels in its own pleasures and desires, and looks to God to bless the plans that we've created to fulfill our own purposes. Some individuals have become so distraught, angry, or disillusioned over world crises—wars, tsunamis, floods, and other natural or human-generated disasters—that they have concluded that there is no God, or at least that God is not concerned with human affairs. As a result, such individuals may assume that life has no purpose or that each of us will have to resolve our existential despair by creating our own purpose. However, neither a self-centered approach to life nor a godless worldview fits with what we find in Scripture about human purpose.

Although church traditions have come up with various syntheses of biblical teaching on the subject, there seems to be universal agreement among Christians that God is the source of meaning and purpose for human life. For example, though he does not speak for every Christian, Rick Warren, pastor of Saddleback Church in Lake Forest, California, has recently brought the issue of purpose into high visibility in the popular culture through his immensely influential book *The Purpose-Driven Life*. Few Christians, I suspect, will argue with his starting place or his primary thesis.

Warren opens chapter 1 of *The Purpose-Driven Life* with these arresting words: "It's not about you."[1] He goes on to explain that our self-centered way of thinking leads us to look to the wrong place for the meaning of our lives—to ourselves. Rather, as human beings, we will find our purpose in life only in God our Creator, who designed each of us uniquely in a way that fits with God's eternal purpose for the entire cosmos.

Yet how often do we stop to reflect on God's purpose for our life? How often are we willing to change what we are doing, where we are going, and how we are doing what we do, out of a sense of desire to align our lives more closely with God's will?

What's Needed

Always seek to serve God's purposes first.

Jesus understood his purpose in this life as doing the will of God the Father. He explained to his disciples, "I have come down from heaven, not to do my own will, but the will of him who sent me" (John 6:38 NRSV). Biblical writers and scholars have summarized human purpose in similar terms ever since.

Rudolf Bultmann, the controversial but internationally acclaimed 20th century biblical scholar, said that most New

Testament writing essentially comes down to helping humans understand who they are in relation to their Creator and their utter dependence on the grace of God. Conversion is an act of surrender; faith is bending our knee to God in obedience, trusting in Christ for salvation, and submitting our will to God's.[2]

"Surrender," "bending our knee," and "trusting and submitting" are appropriate responses for the person who truly believes that our Creator God has redeemed us and has given us eternal life. When we respond to God in these ways, we are saying, "In you alone, O God, is life. I cannot experience this life apart from your gift of mercy to me through Christ. I will let go of every impulse within me to resist you and your will, so that I can receive from you what you are graciously offering to me." Initially, such faith reorients us toward God, so that our minds and hearts are in alignment with all that God has done through Christ to bring us into a right relationship with him. As an ongoing way of life, always seeking to serve God's purposes first is a logical extension of an attitude of submission to God.

But what is God's will to which we must daily submit? God's general will for every Christian is the same; it includes transformation of our hearts, minds, and lives in ways that produce faith, love, and service. God's specific will for each of us varies, pertaining to our calling and unique opportunities to use our gifts and abilities to serve God at a given time and place. For all of us, our purpose in life is rooted in a right relationship with God and in living out God's will—a path that extends to benefit others as well ourselves in various ways.

For me, to love, serve, and glorify God, in communion with the body of Christ, sums up biblical teaching on human purpose well. In other words, to fulfill our God-given purpose, we need to:

- Love God with all of our heart, soul, and mind (Matt. 22:37).
- Serve God by loving and serving others in a wide variety of ways (Gen. 1:26; Matt. 22:39; 25:40; Eph. 2:10; Titus 2:14).

- Seek to please and to bring honor to God in everything we do, becoming more and more like Christ (2 Cor. 5:9; 1 Cor. 10:31; Rom. 8:28-30).
- Live out our relationship with God in communion with the body of Christ—a life that includes being good stewards of our gifts and abilities (Rom. 14:17; 1 Cor. 12).
- Experience the abundant life of love, peace, joy, and fruitful work that comes by being in a right relationship with God and pursuing our God-given purpose (John 10:10; 15:1-12; Gal. 5:22-23).

As leaders, we are called to be devoted to the will of God for our life and to lead within this broader framework of loving, serving, and glorifying God. First, though, we need to be sure that our position of leadership fits our God-given purpose in life.

Aligning Our Leadership Role with God's Will

Bill Hybels, pastor of Willow Creek Community Church in South Barrington, Illinois, once told an auditorium full of pastors and Christian professionals that it is important to be "rock-solid sure" of one's calling.[3] I have not always felt such certainty about a particular assignment, but at the times I have, my leadership has tended to be more confident and better able to withstand difficult challenges. When I'm sure of my calling, I'm not easily discouraged or defeated. I'm rarely tempted to look around for other opportunities, because I have a settled sense that I am where I am supposed to be. I am committed and resilient, knowing that I am doing the work God wants me to do.

However, in the real world of limited job opportunities and other restraining influences, we may diligently seek God's will for us but believe we have to settle for whatever position is offered to us. We may wind up in a position of leadership without a strong sense of calling, passion, or vision.

What happens then? The answer depends considerably on our perspective. If we believe that our position is a provision of God to help us meet our needs and to provide for our families, we may feel grateful. Certainly, from such a point of view, an appropriate response would be to do the best job we can to fulfill our duties and to contribute to the success of the organization we serve.

However, what happens if we no longer sense that there is much connection between God's will and the position we hold? That is, what happens when we don't have (or when we lose) a sense that we are where God wants us to be? We may flounder, we may begin doubting God or ourselves, or we may increasingly serve our own agendas. We may try to make ourselves feel good about our leadership role—a role we don't feel called to—by telling ourselves that God needs leaders to help with this kind of ministry, or to represent Christ in a secular organization, or to serve in whatever capacity we find ourselves. Indeed, we may be doing good work, and Christians are needed in every workplace, but the important issue for each of us under such circumstances is this: are we doing the work God is calling us to do?

Beware. Beware of leading without a sense of calling, or of leading aimlessly; that is, without a sense of God-given purpose. You risk missing out on what God intends for you to do, and the world may be missing out because you're not doing it. You, your staff, and your family may all suffer because you are not following God's leading, because you will be out of sync with God's Spirit, and your attitude and demeanor cannot help but be affected negatively. Your organization may suffer, because someone who is called to the leadership role you hold can't serve as long as you cling to it.

Even if you are in a job because you want to be there, or don't want to be somewhere else, if you are serving your own agenda rather than following God's leading, your actions will be ultimately self-defeating. You may feel guilty or empty, even if you reach your goals and produce significant results. Worst of all, your relationship with God will likely suffer.

If you are struggling with your sense of call to a particular role, you may need to make a change. Perhaps you are being called to something new, and you need to act by looking into new job possibilities or fresh opportunities for service. Perhaps your present role is not adequately drawing on your strengths and passions, so that you believe you are not being a good steward of your gifts. Your heart may be in another kind of ministry. Whatever the cause for your questions and concerns, can you do something about the consternation you are experiencing? Is God calling you to make a change in your place of employment or ministry, or to change the role you play in leadership?

On the other hand, the needed change may be quite different from what you think it is. Perhaps you are being called to change within yourself, particularly in the way you are leading, right where you are. Sometimes our sense of dissatisfaction or restlessness comes from our unwillingness to face the truth about changes we need to make in our personal or work priorities, our relationships with co-workers, our methods of leadership, or the use of our gifts and resources. For example, sometimes we are irritable with staff members because our expectations are unrealistic. Perhaps we are taking for granted what we are able to understand and do without adequately realizing that not everyone has been given the same gifts that we have. Is God calling you to make changes in how you view and work with others, or in some other way related to your thinking or leading?

One of the hardest decisions I have had to make in my life was to leave a leadership role in a ministry I believed in passionately and had felt called to more than a decade earlier. My heart was in the mission and the vision. I had worked hard for nearly 10 years to advance the cause, to increase the scope of our outreach, to add staff, and to create a vibrant, fruitful, growing ministry. However, something was wrong.

Increasingly, I felt I was neglecting my gift of teaching. As the demands for fund-raising and expansion increased, I was being sucked into roles for which I did not have passion, roles that either drained me or simply kept me from the study, writing, and teaching to which I felt called. I did not want to give up my position of leadership, but a personal crisis was looming. Something needed to give. Something needed to change.

After agonizing, sleep-deprived nights, much soul-searching, and prayer, I knew that I needed to act. I began by consulting with some of my closest friends, my spiritual director, my wife, and eventually the board executive committee of the organization I served. I was willing to enter into a process of corporate discernment. I would make myself vulnerable to the board, so that we could seek God's leading together. However, by the time the matter came to the full board, I knew that I needed to announce my decision to hand over the reins of leadership to someone else. I would have liked to stay and continue my teaching and mentoring ministry on the side, but trying to juggle two jobs just didn't make sense anymore, either for the ministry I was leading or for the new ministry I was developing. I needed to make a change, and only one way seemed workable: we initiated a succession process that would lead eventually to my resignation.

We will focus on personal change in a later chapter. For now, these are the main questions:

- Are you sure that your position of leadership fits your God-given purpose in life?
- Are you open to the possibility that the struggles you are having may be due in part to your way of thinking and leading, rather than to the role or responsibilities themselves?
- Are you committed to making whatever changes are necessary to stay in sync with God's will, as best as you can discern it? In other words, are you paying attention to what God might be trying to communicate to you through your experience?
- Are you listening?
- Are you submitting to God's purposes for your life and leadership?

Aligning our Daily Leadership with God's Will

A second aspect of serving God's purpose for our life as a leader, assuming that we belong in the leadership role we have taken, is to align our will with God's in every aspect of our leadership. To align our will with God's will means that we believe and behave as if God is our personal leader and the leader of our ministry or organization. We submit our plans to God's purposes, even if we don't know what they are at a given moment. I'm talking about an attitude of submission. We prepare ourselves mentally, emotionally, and spiritually to lead with integrity, in ways that grow out of our faith and allegiance to God and our calling.

Psychologist Larry Crabb, in his book *Connections*, talks about the alternative to aligning our will with God's.[4] He outlines some purposes of our own that we consciously or unconsciously serve by the way we lead:

- Proving our adequacy (building our own cities).
- Establishing reputations (being fire lighters).
- Keeping safe (being wall whitewashers).
- Pursuing our own pleasure and satisfaction (being well diggers).

As fallible human beings, we all enter into our leadership roles with mixed motives at best. However, we need to recognize that the higher a priority we give to our own agenda, the more we hinder our ability to connect well with God, ourselves, our co-workers, and those to whom we hope to minister. Why? Because when we consciously or subconsciously seek to serve ourselves more than God, we will increasingly become self-absorbed, and we will care less and less about others. It's hard to connect well with those you don't care much about. Our relationships cannot help but be negatively affected by the degree to which our agendas are driven by our own self-interest.

Jesus said, in reference to the competing allegiances of God and money, that we cannot serve two masters (Matt. 6:24). If we give priority to any self-serving goal—be it money, status, popularity, achievement, security, pleasure, or satisfaction, for example—rather than God and God's will, we will find our worship and communion with

God to be increasingly shallow and empty. We may even become hardened, rebellious, and cold.

I raise these issues not to suggest that any of us can reach some ideal state of pure devotion to God's will in our life and leadership, but to help us become more self-aware about our hidden agendas and to pray for the grace to let them go. A helpful prayer is one that asks God to reorient us to true, wholehearted worship of him, and to re-energize us in our leadership role, in sync with God's purposes. Then we need to set out to align every aspect of our leadership to God's will.

What's Real

Aligning our will with God's is an all-encompassing, ongoing process.

Aligning ourselves with God's will encompasses everything from making major career decisions or significant commitments to flowing with opportunities and wrestling with decisions that may seem minor. In one respect, fulfilling God's will for us as leaders includes identifying our spiritual gifts and abilities, listening for a divine calling to a role or position, and accepting that call by taking on specific leadership responsibilities. In another respect, it means responding to the various daily opportunities God presents to us to serve Christ in the midst of our leading. In short, aligning our will with God's is an all-encompassing, ongoing process of submitting to God.

One significant test of alignment with God's will, especially for major career decisions, is to ask whether we have the necessary spiritual gifts for the task at hand—the role we have taken or the "assignment" we have been given by God.[5] For example, those with the gift of administration may prove to be excellent leaders at certain stages in the development of an organization, while creative visionaries, who may be poor administrators, may be extremely influential and fruitful as leaders at other stages. Those responsible for hiring leaders need to determine the stage at which their organization stands, and to discern whether a candidate's gifts fit the needs of the organization at this place and time.

The basic truth is this: God equips individuals with gifts and abilities so that they can fulfill the leadership assignments to which they are called. Assuming we are so equipped for leadership, a particular calling, whether it comes in the form of a job offer from others or an internal sense of vocation, may prompt us to take a leadership role in a specific setting.

However, aligning our will with God's is about much more than making a career choice or accepting major responsibilities. Regardless of our official responsibilities as leaders, God has prepared "good works" for every one of us to do through God's working in us—major as well as minor opportunities for service (Eph. 2:10). We need to be ready to respond to divinely appointed occasions for doing good on a day-by-day basis that may not be part of our strategic plan or noted in our personal digital assistant. As individuals, we are called to seize opportunities (called *kairos* moments in the New Testament) to do good in our private lives and personal relationships, and as leaders, we are called to discern "the good work" God has in mind for the organization as a whole at any given point.

How do we know what God wants us to do? There is no infallible guide to every "assignment" from God. However, our ability to recognize the work we are called to do increases as we seek to be good stewards of our spiritual gifts by using them regularly and accepting responsibilities that maximize our use of them. Also, our readiness to respond to *kairos* moments multiplies as we cultivate the vitality of our connection to God through ongoing prayer and spiritual disciplines.

Basing their reasoning on such passages as Acts 16:9-10, which records Paul's sense of calling to Macedonia, some Christians believe that we should wait until we receive a specific calling before acting. Caution is needed in working on this assumption. It may cause individuals or leadership teams to become overdependent on signs and supernatural revelation. Such criteria are notoriously ambiguous and not always forthcoming. Rather than waiting for unclear signs and subjective measures, often we would do well to make decisions based on

reason and wisdom. God may very well have left some decisions about using our gifts and leadership to our own discretion.

In fact, scholar Gary Friesen argues that biblical examples
of God's specific leading are *extra*ordinary, rather than nor-
mative.[6] Instead, Friesen presents a "wisdom view of guidance"
that emphasizes both God's sovereignty (to accomplish his
will secretly apart from our ability to discern it ahead of time)
and human freedom and responsibility for matters about which
God does not have a specific will (in which case, seeking God's
guidance would be irrelevant). Thus, Friesen asserts, Christians
should follow God's general will for all Christians—that is,
being moral and doing service and exercising freedom, responsibility, and wisdom in decision-making. He assumes that God
delights in Christians' choosing according to their own will in
areas where they are free to do so.

Friesen's thesis provides a corrective to an overreliance on
supernatural leading and direction for knowing God's will.
Friesen makes an important contribution in urging Christians
to focus on God's general will for all Christians as the main
roadmap for life. After all, the preponderance of biblical teaching indicates that God's will for human beings truly is general. Friesen also helps those who might be paralyzed in making
decisions in the absence of any longed-for signs or promptings,
by urging them to use their heads to make good decisions.

Nevertheless, despite Friesen's helpful encouragement to
use the minds God gave us to make wise decisions on a day-
to-day basis, and to be good stewards of our resources, we must
not neglect the important role the Holy Spirit plays in helping us to discern God's specific will for our life. The spiritually
vital person will continually look to the Holy Spirit both in
the big decisions of life and in the day-to-day matters of doing
good work (Eph. 2:10). I have found value in using, both as an
individual and in a corporate setting, an active discernment
process that includes submitting our minds and wills to God's,
praying, and expecting the Holy Spirit to reveal truth, wisdom, and leading in matters of serving God daily. Then, in
the end, when it comes to decision time, individuals and leaders need to base those decisions on the best wisdom they have

been able to discern, along with any other internal sense of God's leading.[7]

Another helpful attitude and practice that will equip us to recognize and respond to God's prompting to do a good work is learning to "expect the unexpected" and to flow with opportunities that may supersede our intentions for the day, event, or relationship. However, flowing with changing circumstances and yielding to God's unexpected leading is difficult for many of us. We might not mind changing course on a moment's notice if it's our idea, but if people or circumstances force us to consider alternatives, we may be much more resistant.

Significant spiritual issues may lie alongside possible psychological and personality explanations for our resistance to God's will, such as fear of failure or overinsistence on reaching goals. For instance, many leaders like to be in control, and we can be very concerned about producing results in the way we envision—perhaps with or without God's help. We may be overdependent on ourselves and on what we can accomplish, or simply resistant if God's agenda and ours seem to be at odds. Whether or not we go to the extreme of Jonah, who had to be swallowed by a whale to face his stubborn rebellion against God's will, many of us are guilty of resisting God's prompting in various dimensions of our life and leadership.

My own resistance to aligning my will with God's usually emerges when I am afraid that yielding my vision and plans will result in disappointment, embarrassment, failure, or loss of a dream. Psychologist Larry Crabb would call me a "city builder." Those of us who are city builders focus on our adequacy; we fear failure more than anything else.[8] We have a vision for and become excited about organizational growth, and then try in every way possible to make it happen, even if God does not seem to be cooperating. In fact, we have so much invested in our success, or appearance of success, that we can be guilty of trying to build and run operations so well that we could succeed regardless of God's involvement! Of course, we may realize consciously that whatever "success" we experience without God's involvement is not success at all; but sometimes our desire to succeed is so strong and our fear of failure so potent that we lose sight of what really matters—offering ourselves to be used by God to accomplish his purposes, in his way, in his strength.

Sometimes staff members unexpectedly leave, key volunteers or co-workers resign, budget crises require cost-cutting, new ideas and opportunities suddenly emerge from someone other than ourselves, the needs of staff demand time and resources we wanted to allocate somewhere else, the copy machine breaks, or the furnace goes out. Whenever something happens that calls for a constructive response on our part as leaders, we need to be ready to flex. Aligning our will with God's in such circumstances means letting go of how we wanted our day to go and seeking to flow with the way God seems to be directing the course of our response. An unexpected turn of events may require exercising patience and understanding, reorganizing, starting over, reconsidering, or yielding to the demands or needs of others—that is, responding in whatever ways fit with the fruit of the Holy Spirit and wise spiritual leadership. The question is, do we tend to flex and go with the flow to align ourselves with the way we think God might want us to respond, or do we cling to our own will and way?

A few years ago, circumstances beyond my control forced me to become more flexible in my own response to the unexpected and to get in better sync with God's leading in situations that I did not orchestrate or would not choose. My staff and I were hosting 300 golfers who had paid $250 each for a chance to play one of two very nice upper-end golf courses. In turn, we were looking forward to having them stay for lunch or dinner to hear a presentation about our ministry, at which time we would do our big fund-raising appeal. Our nonprofit organization counts on significant income from this event. It's an important occasion, but this year I had to learn that something was far more significant than having the day run as I had planned. I had to learn to surrender my reliance on myself and my plans, and to focus better on God and what God wanted to accomplish through the day.

Recognizing my tendency to be a city builder, I prayed beforehand and during the day of the golf tournament for God to help me not to make the day about me, my performance, or my adequacy, but to focus instead on serving God's purposes. However, I was still not fully prepared emotionally for a deluge that threatened to wipe out one or more of our three tournaments that day.

At first, I was distressed, thinking the day would be lost or, worse, that a rained-out event would reflect poorly on me. City builders are so afraid of failure and looking or feeling inadequate that we can leap to irrational conclusions when things don't go right. On that rainy day I started blaming myself. I worried that the event would be a failure, and that ultimately I would be a failure as executive director.

Fortunately, I remembered Crabb's insights, and God's Spirit led me to a better place mentally, spiritually, and emotionally. After the golfers went out in the morning, all the staff and volunteers got together to pray. As the rain was falling, we released our plans for the day and asked God to help us to be ready to serve whatever purposes he had in mind. It was a hard transition for me emotionally, because I was so determined to have the event go the way I imagined, and I was fearful of failure. Yet once I experienced this shift within me, the rest of the day flowed smoothly.

We had to cancel the morning tournament and both of the afternoon tournaments, but the decision led to many meaningful conversations with golfers, who had to stand around the golf shop to keep dry. Some of my co-workers were afraid that only half the people would come back for the evening program and auction, but others held out in faith for much more positive outcomes. As it turned out, we had to add extra tables to accommodate all the people who came for the evening. There was a vibrant spirit in the room, and people were generous. We not only reached but exceeded our financial goal.

Our opportunity, or even calling, on that day was to align ourselves with God and God's will by letting go of our preconceived notions of how the day should go. Instead of rigidly clinging to our plans or depending on our ability to create the perfect experience to achieve our desired outcomes, we needed to ask, "God, what do you want us to do today in light of these unexpected and disappointing circumstances? Where are you at work, and how can we flow with whatever good you intend for this situation?" I have no way of knowing what results we would have experienced had the day gone as planned. Yet I saw the tremendous result of being flexible, flowing with circumstances beyond our control, and maintaining an attitude of faith by looking to whatever good God might have for us to do in the course of the day.

Now, I certainly have other stories about times that did not go as planned, times that we fell short of a financial goal, or lost a valued staff member, or had to curtail an exciting program. At times, I haven't known how to interpret the unexpected difficulty or have felt confused. Sometimes I wonder: Is God frustrating our agenda for some reason? Are we struggling because God isn't involved at all, or are other forces at work? Do we need to work smarter or try harder? Do we need to let our plans go for now and try again another time, or should we abandon the initiative altogether? These questions require discernment, and easy answers or "happy endings" are not always readily forthcoming.

Nevertheless, despite the challenges involved in discerning God's leading and interpreting the meaning of disappointing, frustrating, or scary developments as we attempt to lead, effective spiritual leaders make aligning their will with God's an ongoing daily priority. Without such surrender and willingness to adjust our thinking and acting, there is no point to our entering into a discernment process to seek God's will. After all, why would God reveal wisdom to someone who is not willing to follow it?

James was probably getting at the futility of seeking God's leading without a commitment to trusting and following what is revealed when he talked about doubting:

> If any of you is lacking in wisdom, ask God, who gives to all generously and ungrudgingly, and it will be given you. But ask in faith, never doubting, for the one who doubts is like a

wave of the sea, driven and tossed by the wind; for the doubter, being double-minded and unstable in every way, must not expect to receive anything from the Lord.

James 1:5-7 NRSV

In this context, "doubting" could refer to our being unconvinced that God will provide an answer to our prayer for wisdom, a situation every person struggles with at one point or another. However, I don't think that is the right interpretation of doubting here. The participial form of the verb James uses (*diakrinō*), which most scholars translate as "doubting," can also mean "to make a judgment by distinguishing or differentiating between two things." Thus, James may be saying here that when we pray for wisdom, and then question and debate what to do after God has revealed his will, we are doubting God's wisdom. We are double-minded: one part of our mind wants to know God's will, and another part wants to hold on to our own beliefs and thoughts independent of what God reveals. Of course, any discernment process requires discussion among the leaders to reach a consensus on what they think God is showing them and how best to proceed. But James is addressing something different from listening and discerning with others. James is addressing an ambivalence in those who seek God's leading—a mind-set that makes them unstable and that ultimately undermines their ability to hear from God at all. We might paraphrase James's words this way (italics added to highlight the new wording):

> If any of you is lacking in wisdom, ask God, who gives to all generously and ungrudgingly, and it will be given you. But ask in faith, never *debating within yourself whether or not you are going to act on what God reveals,* for the one who *is ambivalent about following God's leading* is like a wave of the sea, driven and tossed by the wind; for the *one who holds back on being committed to doing whatever God reveals,* being double-minded and unstable in every way, must not expect to receive anything from the Lord.
>
> James 1:5-7, author's paraphrase

When we are double-minded, we are more or less using God as a resource for suggestions, but retaining the right to make a final decision on our own—in which case we should not expect God to reveal anything to us, James says. There would be no point. God offers to lead those who are committed to doing his will. If we are unwilling to align our will with God's when God reveals his will, then we may find ourselves completely on our own to interpret our circumstances and to determine the best course of action. Although our best analysis may lead to a reasonable strategic plan and possibly to "success," what do we truly hope to accomplish without yielding our agenda to God's? We may even do good things that benefit other people, but what might have been accomplished had we listened to God and followed his leading?

Effective spiritual leaders, then, will be committed to aligning their wills with God's, if they hope to receive wisdom from God. They will seek to do so in the big areas of their life as well as in the small details. They will also recognize that aligning our will with God's is an all-encompassing, daily process of submitting to God.

Here's Help

All of us—as individuals, leaders, or ministry or organizational leadership team members—have to find our own ways to align our wills with God's will. Here are a few suggestions.

Pray daily for a heart and mind that are attuned to God's purposes and eager for God's will to be done—not as a tacked-on ending to prayers asking for blessing, but as a regular part of your devotional life. Pride and willfulness, which will probably always be a temptation for many of us in leadership, continually require special attention and prayer.

Be ready to flex and hold loosely to your plans and ideas about how things need to be. I'm not saying, "Don't have vision and don't persevere." Rather, accept that circumstances are sometimes simply beyond our control. At those times, we need to see the unexpected and the uncontrollable as opportunities—opportunities to see God work in unexpected ways, opportunities for ministry and witness that God may have planned for us.

One way to strike a balance between solid planning and going with the flow is to expect the expected *and* expect the unexpected. Plan as if the success of the event or initiative depended entirely upon your strategic planning and execution. Yet at the same time, prepare yourself mentally, emotionally, and spiritually for glitches and surprises, and view them as special opportunities.

As a matter of regular practice, form advisory groups for every new venture to help create a sense of ownership among others and to guard against acting in a vacuum. So far, we have talked very little about the importance of teamwork and corporate discernment in spiritual leadership, both of which are important. Do not expect God to reveal all the wisdom to one person in your organization or ministry, even if that person is you.

Examine your relationship to your superiors. Are you accountable to someone who will help discern God's will for your ministry? To honor God's calling and assignment to leadership, most of us need to submit our will to someone who supervises us or to a board of directors, even when we think we could ram through our plans if we tried hard enough. Try to honor their role, and invite those in authority to take seriously their oversight responsibility.

If you serve a congregation or faith-based organization, invite your team of leaders to pray with you to discern God's purposes. When faced with a challenge, a major change in plans, or a crisis, call everyone around to stop and pray. Once in my organization, for example, when we were having trouble finding and then acquiring a new property to expand our ministry, I invited the board of directors to kneel with me to pray about the difficulties. We asked God to clear the way, according to his will. It was a positive experience of encouragement and yielding to God together. I've led such prayers at other levels within the organization as well when we've felt stuck or thwarted in some way, with good results—both for the spirit among team members and for resolution of the issue at hand.

If you serve as a leader outside a faith-based setting, you can find others who will pray with you from your network of peers or friends. Perhaps a small group of leaders who belong to the same church you do, or with whom you connect through other channels, would commit to meet regularly with you to pray for one another as leaders and for the challenges your respective organizations face.

Something to Think About

Organizational guru Jim Collins, in his best-selling analysis of companies that go from "good to great," points out our need to confront the brutal facts—as leaders, as organizations, and as companies. If I am in denial about a weakness I have as an individual or in the way our team is working together, I'm bound to perpetuate the situation and won't know what to do to improve my life or our team. If we instead face the truth about ourselves and our work situation, we will know better what changes we need to make for both survival and success.[9]

Looking at the brutal facts about your own leadership, how do you respond when threatened, challenged, disappointed, or frustrated? How open are you to letting go of your own agenda, seeking God's leading, and then aligning your will with God's as best you can?

Use your journal, or use the space provided, to reflect on the questions below. The first question after each bullet is the main question to be answered, followed by additional questions to assist your reflection. If you have enough courage to do so, ask your leadership team and other co-workers who will answer honestly to discuss these questions with you as they relate to you and your leadership. Another fruitful way to engage others in reflecting on these important questions would be to discuss them in triads, using the format explained at the end of chapter 1.

- How do I react when my plans are thwarted in some way? (Do I tend to try to make my will happen anyway? Do I pout and sulk? Do I become bitter and distrustful?

Am I able to move beyond my disappointment or frustration to look for the opportunity in the unexpected turn of events? Am I able to trust that God is still at work in my life and situation? Am I able to pick myself up and act constructively in faith?)

- How do I tend to respond when subordinates challenge my point of view? (Is it "my way or the highway"? Do I pretend to listen, and then go ahead and do what I was planning to do anyway? Or do I genuinely listen for wisdom and insight, regardless of who the messenger may be? Do I try to get past whatever negative reaction I may have to pick out the jewels from an employee's words? Am I able to express appreciation for someone's caring enough to challenge me and to engage in problem-solving or envisioning a better future?)

- How do I pray about my ideas and favorite programs? (Is my heart open to change? Am I open to abandoning favorite programs if need be? Are staff members invited to pray with me for God's guidance?)

- To what extent do I solicit honest input from others about what I am doing and the priorities of my organization or group? Where do I need to include others more in the discernment process of leadership?

- Where do I need to grow to align my will more thoroughly with God's will?

SEEKING GOD TOGETHER

Leadership Practice
Create a vital spiritual environment within your workplace.

Soul Principle
God works powerfully as we seek
his activity among us.

I could tell that it was going to be a long, exhausting meeting. I came with a full agenda, and so did several of the committee members. Mine was on paper; theirs were unspoken, displayed on their faces and in their body language.

I had naïvely assumed that we could move through our business, come to consensus about some key issues, and end the meeting having made good progress on some top organizational priorities. However, as the sparks began to fly, I found myself reacting to the members' reactions. I got more tense and frustrated, and angrier by the minute. The others seemed to be equally alienated and upset.

This conflict was *not* constructive. We were butting heads, without the skills or frame of mind and heart needed to resolve the issues. There seemed to be no effective way of working through the aroused, negative emotions to establish meaningful communication, let alone to discern the will of God or make a good decision together.

Ever been there?

What's Needed

Create a vital spiritual environment within your workplace.

Many dynamics affect the work environment, staff relationships, and the quality of team or committee meetings. Mutual trust, respectful communication, a relevant agenda, efficient use of time, clear decisions, and realistic action steps are but a handful of the important components. There is no substitute for good planning and effective execution. Group productivity can rise or fall depending on how well we present our ideas, listen, and honestly consider the interests and views of others.

For many people, warm personal relationships among co-workers or committee members are crucial for working well together. Building healthy, honest, caring day-to-day relationships goes a long way toward setting the stage for productive teamwork in meetings and on projects.

Spiritual leaders also recognize that the starting place for effective management is consciously rooting all work relationships and processes in rich spiritual soil with the goal of creating a vital spiritual environment throughout the workplace. At its core, this activity fosters faith and a dynamic sense of connection to God in every individual and within work teams and committees. It requires developing positive attitudes toward one another and constructive ways of seeking God's leading together. Then, as the team incorporates many of the spiritual disciplines and practices used by the leader into the culture of the organization as a whole, the entire organization is transformed over time. The goal is to seek to experience

God's presence and activity in every aspect of the organization, so that everything from working relationships to processes of discernment, management, and leadership are grounded in God.

Biblical Perspective

According to New Testament teaching, the key to creating a vital spiritual work environment is actively drawing on God's Spirit within ourselves and other team members. For instance, when the apostle Paul counseled churches on their relationships, their common mission, and their ministry to one another, he emphasized the role of the indwelling Holy Spirit. Each member of the group possesses one or more spiritual gifts to be used to benefit the entire body:

> Now concerning spiritual gifts, brothers and sisters, I do not want you to be uninformed. . . . Now there are varieties of gifts, but the same Spirit; and there are varieties of services, but the same Lord; and there are varieties of activities, but it is the same God who activates all of them in everyone. To each is given the manifestation of the Spirit for the common good.
>
> 1 Corinthians 12:1, 4-7 NRSV

Because of the Holy Spirit's gifts, we can expect God to work through each member of our team to act as God's agent to enrich the life of others. Furthermore, Paul likens the church to a body, made of different members, each of which is needed. Not to draw fully on every member limits the functioning of the whole (see 1 Cor. 12:12-25). As a result, we can infer from Paul's teaching that spiritual leaders will want to create a church or work environment in which the Holy Spirit's gifts are appreciated and used as much as possible, and all members of the team are valued because of the Holy Spirit's activity in their lives.

Paul also assumes that the Christians to whom he writes have experienced spiritual transformation in their personal lives, and he counsels them to govern their dealings with others accordingly. For example, he urged the Galatian Christians to live lives that flowed from the Holy Spirit within them:

> Live by the Spirit, I say, and do not gratify the desires of the flesh. . . . The fruit of the Spirit is love, joy, peace, patience, kindness, generosity, faithfulness, gentleness, and self-control. . . . If we live by the Spirit, let us also be guided by the Spirit.
>
> Galatians 5:16, 22-23, 25 NRSV

In a letter to the Ephesians, Paul urges the believers to base the way they relate to others around them on what they themselves have experienced from God. The love and forgiveness they have received, along with the Holy Spirit, should be the basis for their relationships:

> And do not grieve the Holy Spirit of God, with which you were marked with a seal for the day of redemption. Put away from you all bitterness and wrath and anger and wrangling and slander, together with all malice, and be kind to one another, tenderhearted, forgiving one another, as God in Christ has forgiven you. Therefore be imitators of God, as beloved children, and live in love, as Christ loved us and gave himself up for us, a fragrant offering and sacrifice to God.
>
> Ephesians 4:30–5:2 NRSV

Our relationship with Christ can also provide the basis for unselfishness and servant leadership. Paul urged the Philippians to function constructively with one another in ways that grew out of their own spiritual experience with God and Christ's example:

> If then there is any encouragement in Christ, any consolation from love, any sharing in the Spirit, any compassion and sympathy, make my joy complete: be of the same mind, having the same love, being in full accord and of one mind.

Do nothing from selfish ambition or conceit, but in humility regard others as better than yourselves. Let each of you look not to your own interests, but to the interests of others. Let the same mind be in you that was in Christ Jesus, who, though he was in the form of God, did not regard equality with God as something to be exploited, but emptied himself, taking the form of a slave, being born in human likeness. And being found in human form, he humbled himself and became obedient to the point of death—even death on a cross.

Philippians 2:1-8 NRSV

Surely Paul's teaching also provides guidelines for all those who want to live their lives from a vital spiritual core. At work or on a team, we must value and experience personal transformation in ways that overflow into our relationships and set the tone for the group. As leaders, we are called to imitate Christ's loving, servantlike posture in our leadership, and to make unselfishness and service our corporate values.

In addition to explicit biblical teaching on spiritual vitality and Spirit-filled community life, various New Testament narratives illustrate the value of spiritual disciplines and of seeking the Holy Spirit's guidance as a group when discerning God's will. For example, in the early years of Christianity, we read that the Christians in Antioch discerned the will of God in the context of worship and fasting. We're not told many details, but they concluded that the Holy Spirit was prompting them to assign two of their prophets and teachers, Saul and Barnabas, to missionary service:

While they were worshiping the Lord and fasting, the Holy Spirit said, "Set apart for me Barnabas and Saul for the work to which I have called them." Then after fasting and praying they laid their hands on them and sent them off. So, being sent out by the Holy Spirit, they went down to Seleucia; and from there they sailed to Cyprus.

Acts 13:2-4 NRSV

The transferable principle of this biblical story for Christian professionals and clergy in explicitly Christian settings today comes from observing that God's will became clear to the community as members practiced spiritual disciplines *corporately*. The most thorough and inclusive strategic planning processes available today, as helpful as they may be, cannot provide the added value of Christians' worshiping, praying, and even fasting together to better hear from God. Something happens in the process of looking to God for guidance as a group that has the power both to yield wisdom and guidance and to energize and unify the group.

Another New Testament story gives further insight into how ministries can benefit as godly leaders address administrative responsibilities and corporate needs from a deeply spiritual perspective. Through their handling of a practical issue in the early church, the apostles teach us something about priority setting, decision making, problem solving, and human-resource management.

Acts 6 chronicles the controversy in the Jerusalem church arising from perceived inequalities. The Hellenistic Jews accused the Hebraic Jews of neglecting the Hellenistic widows in the daily distribution of food. Intervention was needed. The apostles could have taken over the responsibility themselves to ensure fair treatment of all, but this would have been a shortsighted solution, because they were needed to focus on preaching and teaching for the well-being of the whole community and for the ministry of evangelism. Instead, the apostles invited the congregation to choose people who were "full of the Spirit and wisdom" to take over the work of food distribution. Delegating that task would, in turn, free the apostles to devote themselves to prayer and the ministry of the word (6:1-6).

This vignette suggests multiple principles applicable to leaders in all settings today. First, the top leaders of the church valued their own gifts and calling—namely, prayer, preaching, and teaching—so highly that they were not willing to let themselves be swallowed up in important but lesser tasks. Second, they did not ignore the problem at hand but created a process by which others could be chosen and assigned to address the issue. Third, the church leaders also recognized the importance of both administrative competence (full of wisdom) *and* spiritual vitality (full of the Spirit) in those who were appointed to duties that may not have appeared "spiritual."

Whether or not a Christian professional is specifically assigned to preach and teach, this story illustrates the importance of setting priorities, addressing problems head-on, and appropriately delegating responsibilities. As leaders, we need to know what is most important for us to do and insist on focusing our attention there while not neglecting the broader needs of the organization. We must gather others to create an effective, equitable, and sustainable system to attend to the administrative needs of the organization or ministry. We need also to take responsibility for creating a solid spiritual base among the leaders by choosing staff and volunteers who are known as wise and Spirit-filled individuals.

Of course, to find ideal people to whom we can delegate is easier said than done. Recruiting the right staff or volunteers with the right qualities is one of the leader's hardest jobs. Some jobs have taken me years to fill, and I have reluctantly filled other positions with people who did not meet my standards for either competence or spiritual vitality. But when I've hired in desperation or did not adhere to Bill Hybels's three C's for hiring—character, competency, and compatibility—I've often been sorry.

My own history of compromises does not invalidate the principle. Rather it confirms it. In secular terms, Jim Collins insists that "going from good to great" absolutely requires "getting the right people on the bus."[1] In spiritual terms, we can echo his extensively researched conclusion by saying that, as is appropriate to the setting, the most effective spiritual leaders will foster a well-grounded, vital spiritual environment by choosing the most competent and Spirit-filled staff members and volunteers available. Occasionally, I have been pleasantly surprised by how some people who were questionable choices grew as they became part of our team. Often, though, poor hires or appointments held us back, multiplied problems, or caused counterproductive tension.

Getting the "wrong people" off the bus, especially in Christian settings, can be difficult, since individuals sometimes have an intractable sense of call to their work or can't understand why their supervisor thinks they aren't the "right" people. Sometimes their perceived value by others may be linked to how nice they are or how much others like them, so talk about competence or "fit" for a job is confused by subjective factors. Sometimes the "wrong people" are respected as strong Christians or for being well-meaning, and since the corporate culture rightly promotes being gracious and loving to each member of the team, others may feel obligated to keep the underperforming employee on staff.

Spiritual leaders must remember that their job is to think about the team as a whole and about what best serves the mission of the organization. This rule applies in hiring and firing staff. Having the "wrong people" on the bus hurts everyone, including the individuals who are being kept on without the right calling, competence, character, or some other necessary quality. The right person may be waiting to get on the bus, but he or she cannot until the wrong person gets off or is assigned to a more appropriate seat. We must be willing to let the wrong people go and continue to seek those with the professional competence and spiritual maturity needed to further the cause entrusted to our leadership.

What's Real

God works powerfully as we seek
his activity among us.

The biblical or soul principle behind the practice of creating a vital spiritual environment within your workplace is straightforward: God works powerfully among those who seek his leading as a team. That is, those who look to God to lead and transform them personally and corporately, as they work with others to serve God's purposes, can experience divine leading and provision in significant ways.

Once when we were trying to decide whether to expand the ministry I led, by planting an outreach in a new community, my commitment to corporate spiritual discernment was tested. I had already made up my own mind and wanted to move forward, but new board members and unexpected financial and staff challenges were calling my views into question. I felt frustrated and impatient but finally relented and agreed to slow down and re-examine our assumptions and strategies.

We formed a strategic review committee with multiple goals. We wanted to bring new board members up to speed on strategic thinking, to reassess our key strategies, and to determine when we would be ready to grow as an organization. However, the meetings did not proceed as I anticipated. At first, they were a bit contentious. Members held markedly different points of view, and I felt frustrated, irritated, and defensive as committee members challenged some of my favorite initiatives and assumptions. As the meetings went on, it became apparent that we could not expand our ministry because we were trying to do too many other things at the same time. We were diluting our focus, our energy, and our resources.

I didn't like what I was hearing, because the auxiliary programs we had been developing were largely my creation and fit with our long-range vision. Nonetheless, the more we talked, the more I had to admit that the board members' objections and concerns were valid. I also had to admit that wisdom was emerging that I had been lacking. As we listened to each other, a consensus was forming.

Something was still missing, though. We decided to move the meetings from a local restaurant to one of our conference rooms, so that we could have more space and privacy for prayer. I felt strongly that although we were doing a pretty good job of listening to each other, we needed to listen to God better and to do so as a group.

In our new setting, we began our meetings with Scripture and an extended time of prayer. We expected God to speak through one another, and so we encouraged all to freely express their views, trusting that, over time, the group would be able to discern whether an idea or viewpoint was from God— and wise.

Almost immediately the tone of the meetings began to change. Our ability to listen to one another kept improving. The missing pieces came together. We went from tentative consensus to outright enthusiasm. Breakthroughs occurred as we thought about expanding into a new community; in fact, a couple of members wanted to move faster than I had originally wanted to go. What had started as a tense, unsettled group of board members who were at odds with me and had effectively ground our forward motion to a halt became an energized, coherent leadership team, eager to expand the ministry as soon as possible.

Except for the one board member who resigned.

Our corporate discernment process apparently so irritated this board member that he chose to step down. As much as I like peace and harmony, I accepted his departure as a good thing. His resignation was not a sign of a problem as much as it was an unexpected result of the process that refined our board as a leadership team.

In retrospect, I could have tried to ram through my will when I first proposed expansion. Perhaps I would have been "successful" in getting board approval. Moving forward immediately to expand may even have been the right decision for our organization, because we would have maintained the momentum we had been building. However, pushing my agenda at the expense of creating a broad base of solid leadership for the organization would have been the wrong decision for the ministry as a whole. Attempting to expand at that time may have also resulted in a colossal failure, because our program was in need of greater refinement than I had been able and willing to see.

Some may think that my working through the group to discern wisdom and God's leading demonstrates weakness on my part. A stronger, more capable leader might have known the right thing to do or might have come to the same conclusions far faster. A better leader may have been able to garner support from the board more quickly, without so many bumps in the road.

Perhaps so. Yet what is gained by taking time to listen to one another and to God in a corporate discernment process is priceless. Team ownership and unity, along with depth of conviction and wisdom, more than compensate for whatever time may be lost by working a group process. Some people in the organization may prefer the image of a strong leader. However, I would rather admit my weakness, if dependence on the others on the leadership team is weakness, and let God work through the full team to discern the best course, rather than bully or fake my way.

Humble servants who seek and rely on God's working in and through the leadership team or others in the body of believers can often discern God's leading in ways that they cannot on their own. While bold leadership without consensus is sometimes needed in a time of crisis or special opportunity, there is also a risk of shallowness or foolishness when direction and decisions depend excessively on one person's knowledge, wisdom, and spiritual sensitivity. And there is danger that ego-driven, self-reliant efforts may produce "good" results at the expense of the "better" and "best" results that God intended.

The apostle Paul, himself an effective ecclesiastical entrepreneur and leader, preferred dependence on God's grace and Christ's power within him to dependence on what he could accomplish through his own strength. In fact, he went as far as to "boast" in his weaknesses, because he had learned that the strength he most needed and valued comes from God.

In his second letter to the Corinthians, Paul explained his perspective by recounting a word from the Lord that he had received. He was speaking of himself as an individual, but he offers his own experience to give his readers a principle that would strengthen them as a church body. He was struggling with a concern (we do not know what the issue was specifically) that he wanted God to remove from him. The Lord refused, saying to Paul instead: "My grace is sufficient for you, for my power is made perfect in weakness" (2 Cor. 12:9a). From this experience and others, Paul concluded: "Therefore I will boast all the more gladly about my weaknesses, so that Christ's power may rest on me. That is why, for Christ's sake, I delight in weaknesses, in insults, in hardships, in persecutions, in difficulties. For when I am weak, then I am strong" (2 Cor. 12:9b-10). Paul is talking about his personal life here, but the application to leadership is this: effective spiritual leaders will call the team to seek God and God's working in its midst because they value what God can do more than what they can accomplish through their own strength.

To foster a vital spiritual environment in which corporate discernment may be sought, we need to slow down, humble ourselves, listen to one another, and consciously seek to bring God into the process. We must value what God can do through his power in and through us. Even when we are strong and capable and feel confident, even greater wisdom and strength come from the grace of God, actively at work among us. Leaders and staff need to take the time to seek God together, rather than simply following a single leader, who may or may not be able to discern God's will for the whole group—even if that single leader is you or me.

Here's Help

As spiritual leaders, we need to foster faith and a dynamic sense of connection to God to create a vital spiritual environment throughout the workplace. To this end, I offer a handful of practices designed to help others experience God's presence and activity in every aspect of our organizations, which, when done regularly, if not daily, will yield positive results.

Pray Together. First, prayer with one or more co-workers can be especially significant and meaningful when the setting permits this practice. Leaders can pray with individuals, groups, and board members. Team members can also pray together before, during, and after meetings, as well as during special sessions, such as on days set aside for prayer (see below). Be sensitive to what God appears to be doing in the life of those with whom you are praying, as well as in the organization as a whole. Call the team to be open to whatever God might want to reveal, including significant change. No matter whether your setting is faith-based or secular, you may pray with others for wisdom to work through conflicts with them or conflicts that they have with others, if everyone involved is open to praying together. You may also pray privately for team members, for their needs, for their work, and for your relationship with them—that you may fully honor and appreciate them as people with individual gifts and contributions to make to the team.

Actively love your team members. One of the most powerful gifts you, as a spiritual leader, can offer, no matter where you are called to lead, is genuinely to love your co-workers and staff members. I'm not talking necessarily about a feeling of love, and I certainly do not mean entering into an intimate relationship with co-workers. Loving others with the *agape* love that Paul details in 1 Corinthians 13 refers to how we treat others:

> Love is patient; love is kind; love is not envious or boastful or arrogant or rude. It does not insist on its own way; it is not irritable or resentful; it does not rejoice in wrongdoing, but rejoices in the truth. It bears all things, believes all things, hopes all things, endures all things.
>
> 1 Corinthians 13:4-6 NRSV

In practical terms, begin by showing co-workers respect. Be gracious and caring. Be humble and demonstrate by your actions that you are truly interested in their well-being. Forgive when necessary, and be hopeful about their future (even if you are discussing their termination from working in your organization). Listen to what they are saying, and help them think and pray through what they are experiencing. If appropriate, be ready to reassure, back off, or soften your tone if you see signs of discomfort, anxiety, or intimidation. Look for God's activity in your work together, and not just in the outcomes, so that you can help them to celebrate and flow better with God's movement in their life and work.

Practice the presence of God in administrative meetings. In addition to being sensitive to God's activity in your relationships and work with individuals, make a special effort to notice what God is doing in the context of meetings and group work. You may be accustomed to focusing on the stated agenda—normally a good thing—but God may be doing something you hadn't planned that you won't want to miss. Specifically look for the moving of God's Spirit, and when appropriate to the organization, invite others to be alert to how God may be communicating as you discuss issues, make plans, and converse with one another. I often pray, "God, help me to see what I need to see in the course of this meeting." For example, sometimes I need help to realize that I am not listening, or that an individual is not open to a new proposal, or that we seem to be at an impasse, or that while everyone is agreeing, no one is enthusiastic. Often, until I gain insight into an issue or recognize a negative dynamic in the group, I cannot lead effectively.

Practicing the presence of God in administrative meetings also means entering into the process both as a participant and as a genuine listener. Instead of ramming through my agenda or, having already made up my mind, falling for the temptation to subtly manipulate the process, I seek to remain open to whatever wisdom or leading that may emerge in the course of the discussion. I will put an issue clearly on the table but approach the discussion in a way that genuinely invites the full participation of others. I will ask them to expect that God will guide us together through the process. Sometimes, at the conclusion of a meeting, I will take a couple of minutes to ask the participants to reflect on their experience and to talk about where things seemed to come together, or where they sensed God's Spirit at work.[2] Leaders of organizations in which it would be out of place to hold such a discussion in public might still talk with a Christian colleague at work or elsewhere, or simply reflect on the experience on their own, perhaps by writing in a journal.

Hold days of prayer and fasting. Alongside using the disciplines of prayer and fasting simply for your own spiritual vitality, in a faith-based organization you may also invite the entire staff and board (and congregation, if you're a pastor) to join you in seeking God together in this special way. I've led days of prayer, sometimes with and sometimes without the fasting component, in both congregations and other nonprofit settings. God always seems to speak in meaningful ways to those who participate—for example, by making something important clear to them, revealing an issue that needs to be addressed, giving insight, or deepening their sense of conviction or passion about an idea. Fasting can be especially useful as a tool to help participants become more aware of their hunger for God as well as of their overdependence on all sorts of foods, drinks, and habitual behavior to "fill them up" emotionally as well as physically. Leaders who serve in secular settings may practice prayer and fasting on their own, of course, or they might ask a church fellowship group, Sunday school class, or other small group of which they are a member to join them.

When I lead a day of prayer and fasting, I begin with a group session first thing in the morning to review the purpose, biblical basis, and value of prayer and fasting. Biblical passages are suggested for meditation. Priorities and needs of the organization as a whole are identified to help us focus our prayers throughout the day. The first session, one hour in length, includes time for individual or small-group prayer. Then everyone is encouraged to carve out time during the day for silence and prayer as he or she is able. The lunch hour is a particularly convenient time for many to skip a meal, to reflect on their hunger for God as they feel hungry for food, and to seek a conscious connection with God through Scripture reading and prayer. Labyrinth walks and *lectio divina* sessions are additional vehicles to help participants connect with God on days of prayer.

Days of prayer are most effective when there is widespread participation that includes opportunities for everyone to express his or her thoughts and feelings as part of the experience. At the end of the day, we gather to share our experience along with the day's thoughts or insights. At times I have felt a little anxious about what might emerge from the mouths of others: someone might express a new vision for the organization, make a suggestion for improvement, or offer some other revelation from God that does not reflect well on me. I might also get nervous thinking that someone will stir up negative energy that could hurt the organization in some way.

However, my experience has not borne out these fears. In addition, I've come to realize that it is far more important that we hear what others are thinking, feeling, and experiencing than that we try, out of fear or insecurity, to control what is said. If I'm really concerned that someone's comments may prove counterproductive, I clarify that we have gathered to listen to one another, not to seek corporate discernment or to make major decisions. The appropriate leadership teams can follow up afterward on new ideas or concerns.

Hold extended retreats for staff. Annual, multiple-day retreats for staff members are an excellent way to encourage, nurture, and refresh individuals who have been working hard all year and who may be feeling drained. Retreats also foster a strong team spirit when leaders genuinely focus on meeting the needs of the staff members and on creating a meaningful experience for the team as a whole. If you are serving in a faith-based organization, balance the time between worship, large-group teaching, small-group sharing, and significant blocks of time to play and enjoy one another. The key, though, is to ground the experience in spiritual activity that focuses on God, encourages faith, and promotes consciously connecting to God.

Choose leaders for this event on the basis of their spiritual gifts as well as their position within the organization. It is valuable to have both suitably gifted individuals leading various portions of the retreat and organizational leaders demonstrating their commitment to the retreat by their participation. In one way or another, executives and managers need to demonstrate their commitment to the spiritual well-being of individual team members and of the team as a whole, whether or not they function as the spiritual leader of a retreat or event.

When I am the principal leader of the event, I delegate the logistics of the retreat to others and focus on serving as the spiritual leader. Someone else handles the singing and music, since that is not my gift, but I teach the Bible study and prepare spiritual exercises, journal questions, and small-group guides for each day, because these things fit me well. This time of spiritual teaching, challenge, and renewal has become an important component of our investment in staff.

If your organization requires that you take a more subtle approach to spirituality, you can replace corporate worship and Bible study with other spiritually stimulating experiences. For example, allow time for silence and personal reflection, discuss quotations from well-respected spiritual leaders of various faiths, and encourage individuals to connect to a higher power or life force as they seek refreshment and renewal. Then, outside your workplace, you could ask your fellowship group or small group, or perhaps the church prayer chain, to pray for you as you seek God's guidance in planning and leading the retreat and for the experience of those who participate.

Conduct corporate worship with staff. One of the privileges of serving as a leader in a faith-based organization is that two or three times a year, I am able to gather all the staff from our various outreach facilities for worship and a message. I use these times to emphasize our core spiritual values, mission, and dependence on God. I see it as my job to provide opportunities for the staff members to praise and thank God together and to lead them to a place of corporate devotion to serving Christ, trusting in God, and depending on the leading and working of the Holy Spirit.

Conduct special programs with a spiritual emphasis. When I first began to wrestle seriously with the issue of seeking corporate discernment—that is, working with others to discern the will of God for our organization rather than trying to figure it out by myself—I initiated a special emphasis that we called "Seeking God Together." The goal was to foster a more vital spiritual environment in the workplace, within which we would eventually seek God's leading for the organization. I invited the entire staff to participate.

"Seeking God Together" began as a six-month project that was part of the course "The Soul of the Executive" that I took at the Shalem Institute. This project was a major undertaking that included eight biweekly sessions called "Praying for Deep Change." I wrote monthly articles on spiritual growth and change for our corporate in-house newsletter. I designed five in-depth, multifaceted sessions for that year's annual staff retreat that fit with the theme "Connecting to God." We read four books together as a staff. The intensity of the time and energy commitment limits how often I expect to do something of this magnitude, but it is an example of spiritual leadership that goes outside the bounds of normal administrative responsibilities.

When we finished the six months, I concluded that all of the extra effort was well spent for at least three reasons. First, staff members reported that the books and prayer experiences stimulated new thoughts about God and encouraged them to value their own spiritual growth more highly. Second, I observed that staff members begin to introduce others to spiritual disciplines and to promote spiritual growth among the teens and parents with whom we work. Third, as one senior staff member observed, "Seeking God Together" sent a signal to staff that personal and professional growth in every dimension of life, including spirituality, is a high value in our organization. As staff members grow, so also the organization grows in depth and ability to function effectively to fulfill our mission.

A leader in a nonreligious setting could host a brown-bag (or even simply catered) lunch for staff or co-workers who want to read and discuss a book that promotes personal growth. Spirituality has been increasingly embraced by our culture as an appropriate topic for public discussion, provided that organizational leaders are nonsectarian and inclusive of multiple traditions. Many books and workshop leaders are available as resources to foster significant conversation, to build group understanding and cohesion, to promote individual growth, and to touch on spirituality in broad strokes. The goal for a spiritual leader in a secular work environment is to raise the right spiritual questions, even it is not appropriate to give Christian answers.[3]

Study the Bible together. After the success of the six-month program, "Seeking God Together" began to take new forms. In the fall of the same year, we initiated "Bible Study for Ministry" (BSFM). The direct-service staff and I met together biweekly throughout the school year. At first I led Bible studies, emphasizing how the text we read could apply to the life of a Christian minister and ministry. We also spent sessions studying topics relevant to our work, such as promoting spiritual growth among teenagers, and tough theological questions that affect how staff people think about and relate to God.

Spiritual leaders in a secular setting might consider establishing a "Spirit at Work" group. Group members could take turns suggesting resources from various spiritual traditions and leading discussions about the wisdom that can be gleaned from that tradition for the workplace. These groups would be designed to provide an opportunity for spiritually sensitive co-workers to gather together. The goal would be to learn from each other and to reflect more upon one's own faith and relationship to God in light of others' journeys. Sharing insights, beliefs, and experiences may strengthen commitment to corporate values and create a stronger bond among co-workers. Be careful, though, not to use these groups as platforms to promote sectarian beliefs or to subtly coerce subordinates to agree with you. In fact, it may be best to solicit a well-respected volunteer to organize and facilitate the group meetings.

Draw others into spiritual leadership. The more we draw others into spiritual leadership with us, the more spiritual growth will become a true corporate priority and central to the corporate culture. For example, in our Bible Study for Ministry, various staff members have taken turns talking about their own relationships with God and how they see God at work in their ministry, with the result that their spiritual vitality increases. The staff benefits from hearing additional perspectives and experiences, too. In music, solos can be moving and beautiful, but four-part harmony from the lips of a full choir has a power that can be experienced only when everyone is encouraged to participate. As more individuals participate and use their gifts, the spiritual vitality of the group will increase and staff will experience increased blessings from multiple sources.

To create a stronger spiritual corporate culture, training others to listen to the Spirit's leading along with us is important. Select certain individuals to join you in thinking and praying about spiritual leadership within your organization, with the goals of helping them to grow spiritually and of turning over significant aspects of leadership to those who emerge as especially well suited for the task. The more we include others in spiritual leadership, the more fresh ideas will emerge. We will hear new things, and God will bring the desired vitality in surprising ways. Drawing others into leadership also makes for good succession planning.

In non-faith-based settings, spiritual mentorship of others may take more subtle forms than in faith-based organizations. The principle is the same in both, though: seek others who value vital spirituality, and encourage them to offer leadership wherever and however appropriate.

Fully appreciate the gift of administration as a spiritual and pastoral tool. If you have a gift for administration and you hold a managerial position, view your management as a spiritual role, whatever kind of organization you lead. Expect God to work through your administrative leadership to further the organization you lead and to strengthen the team in various ways. If, on the other hand, you are not administratively inclined but serve in a leadership role, then draw one or more people around you who have those administrative gifts, so that your leadership can be well organized and managed, and you can be set free to focus on your particular gifts. In either case, do not minimize the important contribution of good administration in any organization or ministry, and recognize that through it the Holy Spirit can work as powerfully as through the exercise of other spiritual gifts.

It has taken me a long time to catch on to the spiritual dimension of administration. I understood preaching, worship, teaching, counseling, and caring as spiritual activities, but not administration. As a result, I led meetings using my own instincts and abilities, without adequate regard for what

God might want to do through my management. The result was that I often reacted to those who displeased me from what Paul calls "the flesh"—that is, I would respond from my sin-influenced self by becoming impatient, speaking harshly, driving people, and otherwise treating them in ways that were alienating and counterproductive.[4] Instead of being a gift or a vehicle for the Holy Spirit, my administrative style at times undermined my leadership and my ability to be an effective role model for integrating one's spiritual life and leadership.

At the same time, it was at Family Hope Services that I realized that my administrative leadership was greatly helping the organization, and I was undervaluing it. I came to Family Hope originally to be a pastor to the staff. I didn't really have a clear vision of what that meant, but I knew that I wanted to help make the organization a better place to work for full-time Christian staff members, and I expected to draw on my experience and gifts to make it happen. Surprising to me, I have come to learn that one of the best pastoral contributions I have made over the years has been in the area of administration.

Those of us who have the gift of administration can create structures and processes that are safe and fair for staff members and can provide vehicles for them to receive the training and support they need to be successful. We can lead meetings in ways that draw out the unique contribution of each staff member. We can create mechanisms to use gifted staff members in ways that benefit the mission of the organization and bring greater joy and meaning to the individual. We can ensure that staff members have places to go to talk safely about their concerns and to receive whatever support the organization can give to them.

Administrative work done in these thoughtful and caring ways can be very "pastoral." The result is that the staff feels well cared for and supported by the organization. Job satisfaction, morale, and productivity increase. Such pastoral administrative support prevents staff from feeling exploited, mistreated, neglected, or undervalued, as can so easily happen among clergy and professionals in direct-service work. Truly, a spiritual leader's administrative efforts on behalf of staff communicate that God cares about the worker as well as the work—a key ingredient in fostering a vital spiritual work environment.

Something to Think About

Reflect in your journal or in the space provided below on the following questions. Then invite your leadership team to think together about spiritual leadership in your group or organization.

- What has worked best for me to root my leadership practices and work relationships in a rich spiritual soil?

- What have I learned from not paying enough attention to the spiritual vitality of those I hire or recruit to work with me?

- What could I do to create a stronger spiritual environment in my setting?

- How could I better encourage the spiritual growth of my co-workers and staff?

EMBRACING CHANGE AS A FRIEND

Leadership Practice
Make change a personal priority.

Soul Principle
Change is our calling.

Change is not optional.

At least, change is not optional for those who want to keep growing as individuals and leaders. It's not optional for those who want to become increasingly effective and fruitful in their work and ministries.

Pressing problems in the church call for change as well. The serious state of affairs in many churches—from scandals to declining attendance, division, and infighting—calls for change. The troubling social, political, and environmental issues in society as a whole demand change. Our own pain, distress, frustration, and disappointment in our relationships, work, and ministry all point to the same conclusion.

Either we change, or we will face more of the same—or worse.

You may serve an organization or institution that is "stuck." It may have serious problems whose solutions seem elusive or unattainable for one reason or another. For example, whereas many congregations are truly beacons of light and centers of hope for people, others are centers of judgment and negative energy. Leaders are frustrated and disillusioned, and countless staff members are demoralized, hurt, and angry. Conflict abounds at one end of the spectrum, and apathy or lifeless traditionalism at the other. While a number of megachurches continue to grow, the vast majority of churches are dying—not just because of the competition, but because they are out of date and deemed shallow or irrelevant in a postmodern world that longs for spiritual mentorship and community.[1]

Other churches and organizations may be growing and expanding, yet missing out on God's will for them because of an unwillingness to change. Power brokers are satisfied with the status quo and don't want to change much of anything. Perhaps the credo of their leadership team or board is, "If it ain't broke, don't fix it." However, if God has something else in mind for these organizations and the leaders are not listening or changing, then something *is* "broke." A process of corporate discernment may be needed to determine whether God is calling the organization to something new, but if the leaders are not truly open to God's leading, unwavering devotion to the status quo is another kind of "stuckness."

Leadership is in crisis, too. While many pastors and other organizational leaders are highly appreciated and respected, many others conduct themselves in ways that communicate a low self-image, incompetence, self-centeredness, or lack of integrity. No leader can ever be perfect, but we can set attainable standards for ourselves to win and keep the respect of those who look to us to lead. We can humble ourselves before God and others by not insisting on getting our own way or on glorifying ourselves. We can seek to be well informed about the culture around us, to take care of our minds and bodies, to be thoughtful and fair in our treatment of other points of view, and to be well prepared in our speaking and teaching. Above all, we can be people of integrity who live by our values and hold our staff accountable.

In my five decades of life, I have seen churches suffer from one scandal after another related to irresponsible leadership. Many well-respected pastors have been forced from the ministry and have devastated their families and followers by having an extramarital affair or by committing some financial impropriety. Multitudes of Catholic priests have been accused of sexually abusing children—a scandal that has resulted in convictions, defrockings, multimillion-dollar settlements, and growing cynicism. Change has long been needed, and some leaders are finally responding to the demands of the law and the people to provide better accountability for clergy and safeguards for parishioners.

Whether you are experiencing dismal atrophy, a stubborn commitment to the status quo, closed-mindedness, a lack of integrity and respectability among the leaders, or some other detrimental dynamic in yourself or your organization, how open are you to doing something about it? Is there a dream or vision you have for yourself, your organization, or its leadership that will not materialize until you make some necessary changes?

What's Needed

Make change a personal priority.

What dream or vision do you believe God has given you for yourself and the organization you serve?

Stephen Covey, author of *The Seven Habits of Highly Effective People*, rightly insists that effective people "begin with the end in mind"; that is, they cultivate a dream or vision of who they want to be, or where they want to go, to guide their thinking and planning. What dreams or visions do you have? We all have them. Some of us may have grand aspirations, and others of us have more modest goals. All leaders see something that is not yet a reality—even if only dimly—and want to help bring that dream or vision into existence.

Yet, if we all have them, why don't more visions become reality? We may be hard workers, determined to succeed, but still feel stuck and frustrated. We may have come to believe that our visions more closely resemble mirages than the Promised Land. Many of us desperately want to know what is thwarting our efforts.

Be willing to change.

At the core of many frustrated dreams is the unwillingness to change. We may not want to admit that we've been wrong *all these years*. Sometimes fear paralyzes us—fear of the unknown, fear of losing the gains we have made, fear of failure, and fear of other perceived losses or negative consequences that might result from stepping out to make a change. Sometimes we resist change because of personal weakness, such as laziness, addictions, lack of vision, shortsightedness, or stubbornness. At other times, we may simply feel weary or alone. Often, perhaps, we may know that something is wrong, but simply can't see what ought to be changed and need a truth teller with a fresh perspective to help us see the way forward.

Misguided self-interest may also cause us to resist making the changes needed to pursue the vision God has given us for our lives and leadership. Have you ever shifted your goals and priorities to minimize your struggle or pain at the expense of providing the leadership needed to pursue the vision God has given you? Have you ever let your focus slide from the mission to what you can get out of your employment or position? I imagine everyone has done these things at one time or another. Self-interest and personal comfort are indeed powerful motivators to change, but not in the ways needed to serve God's purposes.

In life and leadership, the right kind of change is required not only to correct problems; ongoing change is also part of what it means to be alive and to keep moving on our spiritual journey in pursuit of our God-given dreams and visions. We sometimes forget that to get from point A to point B, from where we are to where we would like to be, change—sometimes drastic change—must occur. We want great results and good feelings about our leadership and ministry, but sometimes we are unwilling to make the adjustments necessary to get there. Change is simply constitutive of living, serving, and growing in every aspect of our life, but until we begin to view change as our friend—as those adjustments and actions that help us to realize our dreams—we will probably keep resisting it.

In his penetrating book *Deep Change: Discovering the Leader Within*, Robert Quinn stresses the importance of heeding the call to change, despite our tendency to resist it, both for our own sake and that of the organization we serve.[2] We may be able to justify keeping things the way they are for the rest of our lives or tenure in our positions, but failing to address real needs for change leads to distress, stagnation, or deterioration both within ourselves and in our organizations. The more our inner world is out of alignment with our outer world—that is, the greater the discrepancy between what needs to happen and what is actually happening—the more negative will be the effect on our frame of mind. Quinn describes the phenomenon that occurs when we don't make the needed changes:

> As time passes, something inside us starts to wither. We are forced to live at the cognitive level, the rational, goal-seeking level. We lose our vitality and begin to work from sheer discipline. Our energy is not naturally replenished, and we experience no joy in what we do. We are experiencing slow death.[3]

It is not hard to imagine how failing to make needed changes will hurt us not only psychologically and emotionally but spiritually as well. If we say no to God's prompting in our lives, we may develop a pattern of resistance to and alienation from God. Biblical writers sometimes call refusing to make the changes God calls for the "hardening of our hearts." For example, when God commanded Pharaoh, through Moses, to release the Israelites, "the LORD said to Moses, 'Pharaoh's heart is hardened; he refuses to let the people go'" (Exod. 7:14 NRSV). Again, after the plague of hail, we read: "But when Pharaoh saw that the rain and the hail and the thunder had ceased, he sinned once more and hardened his heart, he and his officials. So the heart of Pharaoh was hardened, and he would not let the Israelites go, just as the LORD had spoken through Moses" (Exod. 9:34-35 NRSV). Eventually, Pharaoh's resistance led to disaster—his whole army that pursued the fleeing Israelites perished in the sea (Exod. 14:28).

As Christians, with the Holy Spirit within us, hardening our hearts may not lead to death. Yet resisting God's will can greatly diminish the vitality of our relationship with God. How meaningful can our communication and sense of connection with God be if we have our fingers in our ears? How much spiritual energy will we experience if we keep shutting down the prompting of the Holy Spirit?

No one is saying change is easy. Only leaders know how lonely and difficult it can be to have a vision that others don't share and to carry the weight of responsibility for whole departments, divisions, or organizations. Yet effective leaders will endure the self-sacrifice, pain, and risk involved in fostering personal, professional, and organizational change to pursue the dream. They will do everything within their power to further the mission of the organization, to maintain corporate values, and to uphold standards set for outcomes, staff selection, and work relationships.

Quinn explains, "[Leaders] do it because it is right and because it brings enormous internal satisfaction."[4] Such individuals "are internally driven leaders who are committed to continuing deep change and the pursuit of excellence."[5] We may add, spiritual leaders are willing to make the sacrifices necessary and to endure the pain of making those difficult changes because they are also committed to fulfilling their calling by serving God's will above all else.

Thus, just having a vision or dream for our future is not enough. Nor is it enough, as the leader or boss, simply to demand results. We must also work to create what does not yet exist—a process that begins with our willingness to make all the necessary personal and organizational changes along the way, beginning with ourselves.

Be a change agent.

Often we attempt to identify the "what" that needs to change by focusing first externally; that is, on what is wrong with others, our co-workers, the boss, the board, our job, the competition, or our work environment. Indeed, sometimes change is needed in the system in which we work. Often organizational dynamics must be confronted and altered. Sometimes, we may even need to change our workplace and find a new job.

However, what usually needs to change first—and what is often most within our power to change—is something within ourselves. We may be willing for others to change and may even insist on it, but what about us? Are we prepared to do the painful work of looking honestly at who we are, how we communicate, how we work with others, how we set our life and work priorities, and how we manage our time? How willing are we genuinely to open ourselves up to criticism and to respond accordingly? How honest can we be with ourselves about our strengths and limitations so that we make the changes necessary to focus on what we do best and delegate to others what they can do better than we can?

We may need to learn new ways of approaching issues and people on a day-to-day basis. For example, we may need to become more assertive, less controlling, more forthright, or more tactful. We may need to tackle problems head-on or learn not to be overwhelmed by challenges. We may need to change our priorities, work habits, or relationships. We may need to learn to be less reactive and more constructive in our attitudes and responses to criticism. Here's the issue: are we identifying what changes are needed within ourselves, and then working toward making them?

On the organizational level, many problems have fairly easy or self-evident solutions, at least to the leader, and can be resolved by making incremental changes. Two departments need more meeting space, and someone proposes staggering work shifts or meeting off-site. All the administrative assistants want the week between Christmas and New Year's off, and Human Resources devises a system for taking turns.

At one point at Family Hope Services, we were having difficulty in keeping people informed and ensuring that they felt they were all on the same team, given that the staff was divided among six facilities. In addition to expanding the monthly newsletter, we began quarterly all-staff gatherings and team-building experiences, and we equipped everyone with e-mail. We also formed a development advisory committee that brought together program staff and development staff quarterly to strengthen the interface between departments and to ease tensions. Nothing we did was earthshaking, requiring study groups or consultants; but we made real changes that moved us forward toward corporate goals of strengthening the sense of teamwork and improving our communication. When you know what needs to be done, there's no substitute for simply making it happen.

On a larger scale, incremental changes can be made to promote organizational growth. For example, at Family Hope we had four outreach facilities for 10 years and then decided to add a fifth one. Slowly over two years, we found a site, raised the money, recruited and trained new staff, and expanded the ministry by 25 percent. We did not create a new paradigm or change our philosophy of ministry. We moved the organization forward in step with established systems and practices.

In certain circumstances, far more is needed than incremental changes. For example, one's personal life or leadership may be stuck, or the organization may seem to be at a dead end, going in circles or declining. Such circumstances call for more significant action. That's when we truly need to think creatively and to be willing to change our mode of operation. Quinn points out, "[S]ometimes . . . we need to alter our fundamental assumptions, rules, or paradigms and develop new theories about ourselves and our surrounding environment."[6] In other words, we need to be willing to embrace what Quinn calls "deep change."

Once when we were stymied in our fund-raising efforts, and tensions were mounting over clashes of values and work styles at the corporate office, we had to face the truth that we needed to change personnel in one of our departments. With great anguish on the part of many staff members, we accepted the resignations of half the department—employees who would have been fired had they not resigned. The situation had become a crisis, and our solution produced another crisis for many staff members who remained behind. Nevertheless, it was the right thing to do. The air cleared, the right people got on board, the new synergy was energizing, and we began making progress almost immediately.

Our workplace had an unwritten rule that "nice" people should rarely if ever be let go, as long as their heart was right. Staff tended to believe that any worker who tried hard and was well liked must be a good employee. We needed to take a stand that these individuals' work performance and compatibility with the executive director's management philosophy, values, and expectations were more important than trying to please their friends on staff. We could have stuck with the old system of patiently trying to work with unsatisfactory employees by compromising, appeasing, avoiding conflict, and trying gently to nurture and mentor. But that would have only prolonged the pain and guaranteed a continuation of the frustrating quality of work and intraoffice tensions (especially for those who didn't appreciate how these workers clashed with the corporate culture). We needed to be committed to getting the "wrong people" off of the bus and to seek the right people to put on.

Another example of "deep change": after a 20-year history of an all-male management, we decided to seek out women for top organizational positions. A few women had served on the board, but now we had a vision for being more inclusive and affirming of the gifts of women. We were willing to change our corporate culture by holding "women and men working together" discussion groups and actively recruiting female board members and managers. Change did not come easily, but not because of unwillingness. Rather, in relation to gender issues, both male and female staff members had deeply ingrained ways of thinking and lacked conflict-resolution skills. Eventually, our commitment to greater gender equity led to hiring our first female area director, placing women on the executive team, and recruiting several highly competent women to serve on the board.

In the church, sometimes pastors have the option of changing their role to fit more closely with their gifts and calling. After a dozen years as senior pastor, one leader I know voluntarily relinquished all administrative responsibility for the church and oversight of the staff to focus exclusively on preaching, teaching, and pastoral care. He is now much happier, more outgoing, and more effective in the ministries for which he is responsible, and the church is being better administered. Had he clung to the prestige and power of his former role instead of making the significant change he felt led to make, he would have continued to experience the slow death that was sapping his energy and motivation, and that was holding the church back.

Sometimes embracing deep change means being willing to change significantly long-standing corporate priorities and assumptions to create and pursue a larger vision. A number of years ago, at Family Hope, we adopted a "Big Holy Audacious Goal" (BHAG) of "TreeHouse for every community," even though we were struggling with fully staffing each existing TreeHouse.[7] (TreeHouse is Family Hope's youth outreach program in each community we serve.) That is, we chose to make a paradigm shift from insisting on first providing for every need of current programs to pursuing expansion and reaching as many communities as possible. Internally, reassuring the staff of our continued commitment to support existing programs, and then actually doing so, has been important. However, through strategic planning, prayer, and many discussions involving staff, we moved from being an organization committed to sustaining a thriving ministry to being one that valued self-sacrifice out of a sense of mission. To pursue the vision God gave us, we had to be willing to change, and the leaders needed to be change agents within the organization.

As we make change a personal priority by becoming genuinely willing to change and then by being change agents, we will become more effective leaders. Change helps us to pursue the vision God has for our life and leadership and to realize the dreams God has created within us.

What's Real

Change is our calling.

Undergirding the leadership practice of making change a personal priority is a soul principle: God calls us to change. The more we grasp this truth and eagerly cultivate the changes God envisions, the stronger our foundation will be as spiritual leaders. At the core of our being, God calls us to faith and repentance. As leaders, we are called to become servants.

We are called to faith and repentance.

According to the teaching of the New Testament, our calling to change begins with what God does for us and in us—God provides the means for us to change spiritually and begins the work of change within us. The first and most significant change in a lifelong series of changes that God envisions for us is our redemption. By God's grace, we are changed from sinners without eternal hope to forgiven people with hope.

Faith, then, is the bridge from what God is doing on our behalf to our awareness and acceptance of God's gift of grace. It is our conscious link to a change in our spiritual status and eternal destiny (John 3:16; 5:24). Further, faith itself is characterized by a fundamental change from any worldview or way of life that is grounded in human self-sufficiency or self-centered thinking to a heart and mind that focus on God and God's provision of eternal life.

Faith begins by believing that God has provided eternal salvation not by our achievement but by his grace, through Jesus Christ. Faith believes that we have a new identity that we share with all the children of God and followers of Christ: we belong to God as his adopted children. Faith believes that God's grace delivered us both from the consequences of sin (death) and from the power of sin (bondage to sinful impulses), so that we can live in ways that reflect the character of God through the power of the Holy Spirit within us. Faith embraces our God-given purpose in life to love, serve, and honor God—a calling accomplished largely through loving and serving others.[8]

In other words, such faith must change how we live our life as well as change what we believe about God and ourselves. Biblical writers often describe spiritual change as repentance—both an initial turning away from disbelief to faith and a real change of heart that leads to a change of behavior. Faith leading to repentance produces a life of turning away from sin to follow God's will in every possible respect.

Without using the words faith and repentance, Paul, in his letter to Titus, talks about our calling to change by describing how God's grace transforms the person of faith. Specifically, the grace of God changes our eternal destiny (by bringing us salvation), changes our moral behavior (by training us not to do wrong and to do right), changes our outlook for the future (by giving us hope), changes our spiritual identity (by making us Christ's own people), and changes our values and purpose in life (by making us eager to do what is good). Paul writes:

> For the grace of God that brings salvation has appeared to all [people]. It teaches us to say "No" to ungodliness and worldly passions, and to live self-controlled, upright and godly lives in this present age, while we wait for the blessed hope—the glorious appearing of our great God and Savior, Jesus Christ, who gave himself for us to redeem us from all wickedness and to purify for himself a people that are his very own, eager to do what is good.
>
> Titus 2:11-14 NIV

In other words, God's intention is that we will change in significant ways as we trust in God's provision of salvation and act on the new identity and purpose God gives us by his grace.

In broader terms in his letter to the Romans, Paul alludes to our calling to change by offering a vision of personal transformation. After spending 11 chapters describing how the grace of God brings believers into a right relationship with God through faith, apart from human effort or achievement, Paul then sets out for the Romans a lifelong pattern of appropriate response to God's grace:

> I appeal to you therefore, brothers and sisters, by the mercies of God, to present your bodies as a living sacrifice, holy and acceptable to God, which is your spiritual worship. Do not be conformed to this world, but be transformed by the renewing of your minds, so that you may discern what is the will of God—what is good and acceptable and perfect.
>
> Romans 12:1-2 NRSV

Change, or transformation, is our calling as Christians. It often first requires a change in our thinking—what Paul calls the renewing of our minds. In practical terms, we need to cultivate a trust in God and in God's activity in our lives. We need to believe that God changes us for our good, in keeping with his "good, acceptable and perfect" will. Then we need to retrain our minds to reject false philosophies about life and to replace them with beliefs that flow from the gospel and the Holy Spirit's working in our life.

We are called to servant leadership.

The effective spiritual leader is called to imitate Jesus, who came to serve rather than to be served (Mark 10:45). Practically, this means more change for most of us. We are called to give up our natural inclination toward self-interest—seeking status, power, material gain, or comfort, for example—to do whatever best serves the organization we lead. I'm talking, of course, about servant leadership.[9]

Servant leaders will see themselves as servants of God; they will regard leading as a way of fulfilling their purpose in life of serving Christ with their gifts and abilities. Servant leaders serve their co-workers by helping the whole team to succeed. Servant leaders see themselves as part of a cadre of variously gifted and appointed individuals who have been commissioned to serve the kingdom of God together. Serving may have nothing to do with the particular tasks we do during the course of the day, but it will have everything to do with our attitude toward others and with our way of relating to others in carrying out our duties.

The founder of the Institute for Servant Leadership in Hendersonville, North Carolina, Retired Episcopal Bishop Bennett Sims, differentiates between a leadership "role" and a servant "identity." Leaders may have a high position in the organizational chart, but see themselves more as peers, who focus on "making room for others, truthfulness, empowerment, the exchange of power rather than control, [and] a belief in grace and forgiveness."[10]

Learning to be a servant leader, then, means thinking differently about how we relate to others as we function in our role. Rather than focusing on ruling or maintaining status as the preeminent authority in a given setting, we will see ourselves as having a responsibility (rather than a right) to draw others into a process of discovering and producing the best possible result. Yes, results matter; but servant leaders are concerned about *how* results are achieved and to what extent the abilities of all the players on the team are used, and how people are treated along the way. We are called to serve in whatever ways best fit our gifts, skills, and opportunities *for the sake of* others. Our position may carry more authority than another, but as servant leaders we will see our purpose and status as similar to that of our co-workers: we are all there to serve God and the mission of the organization in the best ways available to us.

In summary, we are called to change—from unbelief to belief (faith), from sin to obedience to God's will (repentance), and from self-serving behavior to servant leadership. As spiritual leaders, we are called to embrace a change of heart, mind, and behavior as part of our ongoing calling to be transformed as Christian individuals and as leaders of a team or organization. We need to embrace our calling by making change a priority in our life and leadership, and accept our role as change agents.

Here's Help

Change is not only our calling as effective leaders. Change can also be our friend, because it is the key to realizing our God-given dreams and to fulfilling our purpose in life. Personal transformation is the way we move from who we are to become the persons and leaders God intends us to be. Change is also the way we move our organizations from where they are to pursue their mission and vision.

Practically, to change so as to grow into the leaders God has called us to be, we need as much help as possible, no matter how talented or strong we may be on our own. The good news is, there's plenty of help available.

God's already helping.

A call to change need not be burdensome or frightening, because it is actually a sign that God is already at work in our life. When we hear a call to follow a dream or vision, to make a course correction, or to change how we are leading and serving, it is a positive sign that God is urging us further along the path on which he has led us. A call to change is a call to embrace the good work God is doing in our life to help us to fulfill our purpose in life. Thus, change of self is not something that we have to make happen by our efforts alone. The changes that God envisions for us are initiated by God's Spirit at work in our lives to enable us to follow his leading, consciously or unconsciously.

Beginning with our vision for a better life or greater organization, God is the author of the changes taking place within us. God is the one who plants the good visions in our hearts and minds, God alerts us to the need for change, and God is the one who is at work in us leading us to a better place. Not every idea or dream we have necessarily comes from God, but the ones that do are worth pursuing, and God will help us to make them a reality.

As discussed earlier, the first and most significant change that God envisions for our lives is God's work of redemption in us. God brings about the change in our status from sinners without hope to forgiven people with hope, apart from our own efforts and inclinations (Eph. 2:8-9; Rom. 3:21-24; 6:23). Through faith in Christ's life, death, and resurrection, we may move from existential despair, emptiness, sin-ridden guilt, or the felt absence of God in our life to peace and joy. God produces a change from ignorance or disbelief to faith in Jesus Christ as our Savior.

Then, once we begin to live lives of faith, God continues to work positive changes in our lives through our life's experiences, especially our sufferings and trials. Paul explained to the Romans that God uses our difficulties to produce positive outcomes, "knowing that suffering produces endurance, and endurance produces character, and character produces hope" (Rom. 5:3-4 NRSV). In his letter to the Philippians, Paul also assures believers that the good work God began in them (as individuals and as a community) will be completed (Phil. 1:6). He seems to have in mind both their eternal salvation and their sanctification; that is, their being made more like Jesus, filled with love, purity, and blamelessness, as Paul's prayer for them indicates:

> And this is my prayer, that your love may overflow more and more with knowledge and full insight to help you to determine what is best, so that in the day of Christ you may be pure and blameless, having produced the harvest of righteousness that comes through Jesus Christ for the glory and praise of God.
>
> Philippians 1:9-11 NRSV

God is the prime change agent in the life of believers, both as the initiator of faith and redemption and as the one who completes the process of sanctification in us. In other words, God is dynamically involved in the lives of believers to produce change in ways that fit with God's will. God is the one who "works in [us] to will and to act according to his good purpose" (Phil. 2:12 NIV). God's Spirit leads believers away from their sinful impulses toward the life God intends for us.

Thus, Paul urges believers to "keep in step with the Spirit," which means living a changed life (Gal. 5:25 NIV). Instead of yielding to the temptation to sin, as we may be more or less accustomed to doing, the Spirit helps us to experience freedom, godliness, love, joy, and the other fruit of the Spirit (Rom. 8:5-11; Gal. 5:22-25), which are at the heart of the abundant life Christ intends for us. God was at work in us long before we had a clue that we needed God or needed change. Our part is to believe in the vision God has planted in our hearts, and to trust that God is actively helping us to identify and make the changes needed to pursue the vision. Then we must act in ways that flow from what we sense God is doing in our life.

Try slowing down.

I've noticed that making changes is particularly hard for me when I'm juggling multiple balls at once, my schedule is packed, and I'm racing along at a million miles an hour. My life or work may not be going well, but I'm driving hard and working as fast as I can to produce results. The problem is that I sometimes wind up not getting the results I want and incurring a number of undesirable consequences.

I've learned at times like that to slow down. Even when I'm feeling a great deal of pressure to make quick decisions or to get more work done, if I'm sensing that something is wrong, I need to call a time-out. I need to pay attention to what I'm experiencing or to the reactions of others.

Slowing down allows us to hear the voice of God, our own "inner voice," and the voice of the organization we serve as leaders. Spiritual disciplines, which include stilling our mind, help us to listen to our heart and gut, as well as to God. We may need to open our mind and close our mouth, so that we can let in what our co-workers and other constituents are perceiving and saying.

We need to slow down our fast-paced daily race long enough to see what we need to see and to hear what we need to hear. Whether we tend to be task-oriented or people-oriented, often it helps to step out of our routine for a few minutes, a few hours, or even a few days, to look and listen for what we have been missing.

Listening is discussed in more detail in chapter 7. For now, the main point is the importance of slowing down long enough to take appropriate steps to bring hearts, minds, guts, goals, processes, and people into better alignment with one another. You may feel awkward as you pause to listen carefully to others. You may think that you are wasting time or going nowhere. However, the result will be greater clarity and power. Here's how Quinn describes the need for slowing down to listen:

> Discovering the inner voice of the organization helps un-cover a vision filled with resonance. To accomplish this task, an individual or group must be willing to break the logic of task pursuit. Preparation, reflection and courage are neces-sary in order to hear the inner voice. The inner voice will provide direction if people have the courage to listen and the commitment to change.[11]

Prayer helps.

On many occasions I have worked hard to make something happen, only to feel stymied over and over again. In such circumstances, I tend to get frustrated and want to push harder and harder. However, I have been learning that sometimes what I most need to do as a leader is to let go. The best course of action may be to let go of a cherished idea, desired out-come, staff member, or process, even though it may at first be gut-wrenching to do so.

At such a difficult crossroads, I have found prayer particu-larly helpful—not necessarily asking God to give me strength to keep battering down the barriers, but to yield to whatever his will may be. We can learn from Jesus, who, when he faced the prospect of brutal mistreatment at the hands of the Ro-mans and a grisly death on the cross, was willing to tell God, "[N]ot my will, but yours be done" (Acts 22:42 NIV). Instead of praying for our will to be done, we can simply pray for God's will to be done—even if we do not know what it is.

When we're ready to go one step further, we can pray for wisdom to see what we have not been seeing and for grace to accept the truth we have been avoiding. Then we can pray for our will to be transformed to align with God's, so that we may genuinely desire the effects God desires. In particular, I created a prayer that I highly value in times when I sense that change is needed. It goes like this:

Lord, please give me eyes to see what I need to see,
courage to face the truth, and
strength to act on what is revealed.

Once we were on the verge of launching a new program to complement our existing outreach to youth. Everything seemed to be in order, except that we could not agree on how the new program was to be integrated with the existing program. The creator of the program and I went round and round. Each of us was frustrated and couldn't understand why the other wouldn't budge. As I stepped away from the immediate situation to pray for insight, I began to see that the issue had more to do with control than with anything else—we both wanted it. I knew I needed to make some compromises, which I did. But it became apparent to me that this otherwise highly valued staff member seemed unwilling or unable to compromise.

Before entering what turned out to be the final attempt to find a win-win solution, I prayed for eyes to see what I needed to see. As the meeting progressed, it became clear to me that my colleague was unwilling to settle for any solution other than the one he proposed. A sinking feeling descended on me, because what I was sensing was contrary to what I wanted to happen. Yet, at the same time, I realized I was being given an answer to my prayer. As painful and stressful as it was, I became convinced that our dream was not going to become a reality. I would have to let it go—and let the staff member go as well.

As you struggle with change, ask God to renew your passion for the dreams and visions planted in your heart. Ask God to remove your fear of change and to show you what you need to face. Ask God for comfort, courage, wisdom, strength, and grace to make the changes called for now. (See Col. 1:9-12 for a helpful example of a prayer for God to produce positive changes within us.) Thank God for bringing you to this point in your life and for the hope he gives you for what is still ahead.

Something to Think About

I grew up a *Star Trek* fan. The stories of the USS *Enterprise* and other spaceships flying through the galaxies, facing alien forces, and rescuing desperate populations captured my imagination. They often made me pause and reflect on my own beliefs and assumptions about life and leadership. One episode of *Star Trek: The Next Generation* made me think about my tendency to want to control my environment and to resist change.

The crew of the *Enterprise* discovered a human colony on the remote planet Moab Four, in the region of outer space known as Moab. Eight generations earlier, colonists had traveled there to create a perfect society in which everyone was genetically engineered. It was a utopia—offering the perfect life and ideal community.

As the story unfolds, the *Enterprise* crew must contact the people of Moab Four to warn them of a great danger that threatens to annihilate the whole planet. However, the colonists do not want any contact with the *Enterprise.* They don't want anything to interfere with their "perfect" world, anything that might upset the balance they have created in their life.

Unfortunately, they really don't have a choice. The danger is coming, and something must be done. Eventually, the leaders realize this necessity, and they allow the crew to land to devise a strategy to save the planet. Inevitably, the crew begins to mix with the local population, and unexpected things happen.

First, several of the colonists express their suppressed long-ing to move beyond their perfect little world. Then, the solu-tion to the impending disaster turns out to be a technology devised by earthlings to help a blind person see, something the colonists would never have discovered since they had cho-sen to give birth only to offspring without "defects." Their society had never had occasion to develop the advanced tech-nology known to the *Enterprise* crew.

Eventually, as is to be expected, the planet is saved. How-ever, the real impact of the rescue is left an open question. The story ends with the colonists grappling with the conflict they feel over whether to maintain their perfectly balanced world. They can keep the status quo and reap the currently experienced benefits. Or they can relax their grip on the con-trols of their life and colony. They can take the risk that the benefits of the changes that would take place—greater knowl-edge and more personal satisfaction as a result of greater free-dom—would exceed the costs and negative consequences that would inevitably result.

What kind of organization do you want to lead? One whose vision is so small or risk-averse that you can pretty much guar-antee reaching your goals year in and year out? Or are you willing to create a God-sized vision, as called for by pastor and author Henry Blackaby—a vision that cannot possibly be ful-filled in your own strength, full of risk, and full of wonderful possibilities?

Reflection Questions

Deep change is critical at certain times in the life of a leader who wants to avoid slow death. It begins by learning to listen, and ends only when we actually take action on what we dis-cern to be the truth we need to face. In your journal, or in the space provided below, reflect on the following questions. In-vite your leadership team to discuss these topics. Use the triad format introduced at end of chapter 1 to help team members think more deeply and to strengthen everyone's ability to lis-ten carefully to one another's answers.

- When I think of a time when I (almost) experienced "slow death" as a result of lack of alignment between my inner self and outer world, what made it hard for me to listen and respond to my inner voice's call for change?

- What can I do to "break the logic of task pursuit" (the routine pattern of my life or work) to set aside some time to reflect, pray, listen, and summon the courage to change?

- What change is God producing in me right now or calling me to that requires my eager engagement and cooperation?

- What do I imagine will have to take place in my life to free me to pursue one important vision or dream I have in my heart?

LISTENING WELL

Leadership Practice
Lead by listening well.

Soul Principle
The Holy Spirit speaks and works
through every team member.

"You have a way of getting what you want," my friend said to me. At first, I thought it was a compliment, but then I wondered. Was I being admired for my ability to get results, or was she resentfully suggesting that I keep pushing my agenda until everyone else caves in?

"You're a take-charge kind of guy," another person once remarked. Did she appreciate my initiative and leadership or was she sarcastically reproaching me for being domineering and "taking over" groups?

"You certainly are tenacious," a co-worker exclaimed after a couple of months of trying unsuccessfully to resolve a difference of opinion. My immediate internal response was, "Thank you!" Then I thought, "Or did you mean to say that you are ticked off that I am so unyielding that I won't compromise and consider the opinions, interests, and perceptions of others?"

Those of us who are CEOs, executive directors, senior pastors, or high-level administrators often have the reputation of being strong-willed and domineering. The same characteristics that contribute to our success can also be resented, annoying, or downright offensive to certain people under some circumstances. We can hurt others and communicate messages that run contrary to biblical values and teaching.

While leaders are accustomed to drawing on various qualities, personality characteristics, and abilities that serve them well in their leadership, to be most effective they also need to be humble and self-aware enough to consider how well they are working with others. We should not assume that we will succeed as leaders merely by "being ourselves," if we mean by that that we don't have to care how others feel about working with us. We are part of a team of co-workers, staff members, or volunteers who not only have feelings but have much to contribute to the success of the enterprise, if they are sufficiently respected and heard, and if their talents are used.

What's Needed

Lead by listening well.

Highly effective organizational leaders remember that success is a team effort. To assume that just because we are the leaders we have all the answers or that somehow don't need others to assist us in decision-making is shortsighted, not to mention arrogant.

Successful leaders not only blaze trails; they also draw others who have the right calling, gifts, interests, and passions to team up with them to serve the organization's mission. Sometimes the best leadership at times requires submitting to or following others on the team who know better what needs to be done. We need to see others on the team, whatever their place on the organizational chart, as co-workers. Each member of the team has unique contributions to make to strengthen the entire team and to add to the fruitfulness of the endeavor. Without each contribution the mission would suffer. We need to tap into the potential of each team member to create a synergy among staff that management expert Stephen Covey describes as not 1+1 = 2, but as "1+1 = 3 and more."

Practically speaking, assuming we have the right people on the bus, we can show that we affirm and appreciate the staff by becoming excellent listeners. Listening leaders will also solicit the wisdom and insight of team members and others to take full advantage of the unique knowledge, experience, and perspective each valued co-worker or stakeholder has to offer.

Listening is a skill we need to apply in every conversation, but we can also intentionally create structures and opportunities for all staff to be heard and to make their best contributions. We can establish the equivalent of the suggestion box (anonymous opportunities to share good ideas); we can include staff at all levels within the organization in strategic planning; and we can form focus groups to discuss proposed policy changes or, better yet, to offer their own suggestions for how best to address departmental or corporate problems.

Once when Family Hope was considering moving corporate offices, we gathered all of the administrative assistants together to solicit their input—after all, they work in the office and use the space more than most of the executives. When coordinating phone coverage and time off around holidays became a problem, management made several frustrating attempts to dictate solutions. Finally we asked the administrative assistants to work out the problem. They came up with a better solution than the executives had, and everyone affected by the decision was happier and more cooperative.

Just as you and I have an inner voice that whispers the truth to us about ourselves or about things that matter to us, so do those who work with us, and so does our organization, church, or team as a whole. Robert Quinn argues that when leaders become listeners, they can hear the inner voice of others and the organization—an insight that allows them to take into account the knowledge and experience of their co-workers.[1] As the voice within us as individuals is often a reliable guide to truth and wisdom, so it usually is for an organization as a whole, and the insight of the group can be greater than that of an individual.

You've heard it said, "Perception is reality." If staff members perceive there to be a problem, there *is* a problem, at least until the leaders have taken time to listen and work through it with them. Sometimes the leader sees the solution, but often staff members who are closer to the "action," to the client, or to the production of goods or services, can come up with practical solutions to challenges that executives or higher-ups might never think of. Thus, listening well to all the insightful voices can be helpful in leading the team to fulfill the organization's mission, especially in a discernment process that may lead to significant change.

Tragically, we often are not listening.

Frequently, we don't listen well primarily because we are too wedded to our own ideas, dreams, preoccupations, ambitions, and goals. We wind up using our power to force or try to persuade everyone else to think and act our way. We may do so out of a genuine desire to further the mission, but our methods may guarantee our failure.

Many times, if we fail to listen and instead try to force change on others, they will resist. Either they will argue and voice their opposition openly, or they will subtly or not so subtly undermine the new initiatives. They may ignore our directives, or they may agree among themselves behind our backs that the new idea is stupid and won't work. They may deliberately do the opposite of the new plan, or they may unconsciously or consciously subvert its success to justify their opinion that it was a bad idea.

We've probably all had the experience of thinking that everyone was on board with one of our ideas, only to have it undermined as we tried to go forward. Yet I've learned that leadership does not have to be so frustrating. The more we learn how to listen effectively—so that others feel respected and heard, and we embrace new thoughts and perspectives — the more the right doors will start swinging open, and the wrong doors will close. That is, by listening carefully to team members, we will better discern the best path to take, our wisdom will grow, and others will more likely cooperate and follow.

Sometimes we can get an accurate understanding of practical realities only from those who have more experience or a better frame of reference than we do. By being teachable enough to learn from anyone who speaks the truth we need to hear, regardless of the speaker's age, gender, race, or position in the organization, we can often save ourselves and our organization from wasting time, energy, and other resources on a bad idea. Besides, the more we are willing to let go of unworkable ideas, the more others will trust and respect us; and, again, the more likely they will cooperate and follow.

How Well Do You Listen?

Effective listening is about two things—attitude and skills. Attitude is foundational. If others sense that we are not open to learning from them, all the skills in the world won't matter. But some of us who do want to learn from others still may stumble in relating to others, because we don't have adequate listening skills.

Think back on the process you used to reach a decision that has not gone over well or has not been embraced by your board, staff, or other constituents. How well did you include those who were most affected by the decision? How open were you—truly—to input from others? Were you open to learning from and even being changed by others? Who did most of the talking? You may have invited others to talk, but if your co-workers sensed that you were not truly listening or that it wasn't "safe" to disagree, they were not going to bother participating in any meaningful way.

Sometimes we inadvertently (or intentionally) send messages that we are not truly interested in others' views. For example, we may have a history of not incorporating others' ideas into our decisions. We may look bored when they talk.

We may interrupt when others speak, fail to clarify their ideas (indicating that we don't really want to know what they mean), fail to encourage them to say more, fail to explore concepts further (to demonstrate genuine curiosity and openness to new possibilities), or continue to present our views as if others had never spoken or offered a contrary point of view.

Do you think I'm making this up? It happens all the time. Many leaders seem completely unaware that they are doing most or all of the talking or that they are not fooling anyone by pretending to listen. They are subtly or not so subtly communicating, "I don't really care what you have to say."

Be Committed to Listening

It can be hard work to create a constructive process, formal or informal, in which the inner voice of the organization and the voices within it may freely emerge; but it is well worth the effort.[2] The alternative is usually frustration, disappointment, unresolved conflict, resentment, and failure. Few workers are going to keep trying to express their views if they think there is nothing to be gained, or that they are committing professional suicide by persistently voicing their true feelings and ideas to a boss who doesn't seem to want their input. When that happens, though, everybody loses. The leader misses out on the wisdom of others, those who don't speak up may become demoralized and unfulfilled in their work, and the organization is weakened and becomes less effective.

To listen well and effectively requires a number of attitudes and actions. First, good listeners hear what the other person says with an open mind. We need to be willing to set aside everything we think we know or think the speaker knows, and everything we want, and communicate that we are genuinely open to be changed by what we hear. We have to discipline ourselves not to think about something else or about our next point while someone else is talking. Our goal is to understand that person's point of view and its merits, and to be moved or persuaded by whatever truth he or she expresses.

Second, effective listeners communicate that they have truly heard what others are trying to say. If others do not believe that their ideas have been understood and respectfully considered, they become less inclined to listen to the leader's ideas or to contribute constructively to any decision-making process. This reality explains why one of Stephen Covey's seven habits of highly effective people is "Seek first to understand before seeking to be understood."

On the surface level of listening, we can parrot back the same words the other person used to demonstrate that we heard what he or she said, provided we do not come across as patronizing. This is what therapists do when they practice "reflective listening"—a technique that helps us to focus on what the other person is saying (whether we initially agree or not), and that helps the other person feel heard. In my experience, others will often keep repeating themselves until they are convinced that I have truly heard them. Sometimes, simply reiterating someone's exact words will allow the conversation to move forward. For example, you could respond to a team member who is concerned about your organization's building a new facility by parroting back the words you just heard: "So you think *this is not the right time to build a new facility, because we can't afford it right now.*" Or, if repeating the full sentence feels too awkward, pick out the key words and repeat them: "You're saying we can't *afford* to *build right now.*"

To go deeper in our listening, we can paraphrase what we have heard. By rephrasing, we communicate that we have not only heard the speaker but that we understand the speaker's meaning. In the instance of the team member who thinks, "*This is not the right time to build a new facility, because we can't afford it right now,*" you might respond: "You're concerned that if we go ahead with the building project right now, we'll be getting in over our heads financially."

When we use our own words, though, we need to verify the accuracy of our perceptions of others' meaning (both thoughts and feelings). Others may shut down or become frustrated if they think we don't understand or, worse, are trying to manipulate their thinking by using different words. Thus, we will be most effective when we use a tone that communicates that we genuinely want to understand and that we want to know whether we have understood. We need to ask the other person to confirm that what we think we heard is indeed what he or she was trying to say. For example, in this situation, we may paraphrase and then ask a question that allows the other person to confirm, clarify, or redirect our thinking. We might say, "You're upset because you think we would be overextending ourselves financially if we were to go forward with this building. Is that right?"

To reach the deepest level of listening, we need to catch what is being said nonverbally and what the person is choosing *not* to say. We need to learn to "read between the lines" of what people say. What do we sense from tone of voice, choice of words, body language, and other nonverbal clues? Perhaps they are exasperated because we don't understand. Perhaps they are frustrated with themselves because they can't communicate what they're truly concerned about. Perhaps they're nervous about disagreeing with us.

If we detect from nonverbal clues such as folded arms or a red face that the person feels angry, frustrated, or afraid, but we're not sure which or why, we might seek clarification: "You seem angry about this proposal." Pause for a respectful interval, and if the person doesn't respond, gently prompt, "Is that right? Or are you feeling something else?" Then, if we're still not sure why the person is feeling that way, we can say, "Tell me more about what you are thinking." Depending on how the conversation is going and how much information the person is giving us verbally and nonverbally, we can also tentatively offer our own perceptions: "I wonder if . . ." or "It sounds as if some part of this proposal just isn't working for you personally. Can you help me to see this situation through your eyes?" And so on.

We can also offer suggestions about others' feelings, if they seem unable to articulate them. "I wonder if you're feeling...." To come across as a psychotherapist or in a judgmental way would be counterproductive. But if we can gently offer some leading options from our perception, such as anxiety, fear, insecurity, or another feeling that seems to match what they are communicating and fits the situation at hand, we may help the resistant one to gain insight. The idea is to clarify what the person is thinking and feeling and to demonstrate that we understand what he is saying and what he means while still leaving things open, so the person can go wherever he wants in the conversation. The team member may not be angry, even though she says she is. Or, even if she is angry, she may not be ready to talk about it. But when we notice feelings and nonverbal communication, we communicate that we are truly listening and that the other person's experience is important in our dialogue with her.

At this deepest level of listening, we're offering back to the speaker thoughts and feelings he or she did not clearly express, to see if we are picking up on something that the person could not articulate. When we do this type of listening well, people will often learn from our reflection: "Yes! That's what I meant. I just didn't know how to say it." Or people will become clear about their feelings: "Yeah, I did feel pretty angry." They may also feel relief at finally identifying the powerful feeling affecting them.

The exact wording of our observations or our questions to seek greater clarity is less important than the clear communication that we are listening, and though we are not sure we fully understand, we want to. Listeners often make the mistake of assuming that they understand what the other person is saying and they rush forward with their counterargument before the other person is certain that he or she was heard. We need to be patient enough to help others gain greater clarity about their own feelings and thoughts, and to wait until they are reasonably convinced that they have been heard and understood, before proceeding to offer our own views. Only then can we expect to work constructively through conflicts or hash out divergent views. When the other person feels heard, he or she becomes much more ready to continue the discussion and may welcome an invitation to help assess whether the organization truly can afford the new facility. How great are the risks? What are the costs of not building? What alternatives might be considered?

To recap, listening well requires maintaining an open mind as we listen and communicating back to others that we have truly heard and understood what they are trying to say.

Then, third, effective listening leaders will take into account the views expressed. If I strongly disagree with someone, I will explain why. If I agree, I will affirm the view and give the one who brought it up credit for a good idea. If I don't know what to think, I will simply say so. If I am facilitating a group discussion, I will try to keep all of the leading ideas that have emerged in front of the team, and work together to establish a process by which a decision will be made. (Sometimes we wait until there is consensus, sometimes the majority rules, sometimes I make the decision, and sometimes we defer to someone who is more knowledgeable or experienced in the matter at hand.) When we are reviewing options, I won't belittle anyone's view or forget to include it, if the group has not already dismissed it.

Sometimes the demands of participating fully in a discussion on a significant or highly emotional issue *and* functioning objectively and fairly as a facilitator are too much for one individual. At such times, we can draw on someone else (from within the organization, from the board of directors, or a professional) to facilitate the discussion. The times when we are conducting strategic planning sessions and fielding employee grievances are especially appropriate occasions to bring in a third party.

The more you can truly listen in these ways, the more you will see positive results:

1. You and the organization will benefit from the wisdom of the team.
2. Team members will feel heard and be much more likely to own the final plan.
3. Your listening well will establish respect and openness as corporate values, and team members will learn from your example how to listen better themselves.

4. Others will respect and trust you more, and, as they become good listeners themselves, their respect and trust for one another will increase.

Management guru Peter Senge, in his seminal work on the "learning organization," stresses that companies excel and leadership teams thrive when executives learn to communicate, to collaborate, and to be humble enough to learn from others' experience and thinking. Successful leaders in growing organizations will even reduce hierarchy for the sake of working and creating together.[3] In other words, Senge agrees that effective leaders truly value the full participation of the whole team, which means that they must learn to listen well.

What's Real

*The Holy Spirit speaks and works
through every team member.*

Listening well is key to good relationships and leadership. As best-selling author, international business consultant, and workshop leader Stephen Covey insists, highly effective people will seek first to understand (what others are communicating to them) before seeking to be understood (by others).[4] First, we need to listen to our co-workers and other constituents because they have important things to say to further the mission of the organization. Second, if team members don't feel heard, not only will they feel disrespected; in addition, a whole host of negative consequences may ensue.

From a commonsense point of view, it would stand to reason that an organization is going to be at its strongest if it is fully drawing on every resource within it, including all the helpful insights, skills, personalities, and relationships that staff and other constituents have to offer. Whether we lead in a faith-based organization or a secular one, we will be most effective as leaders when we value the contributions of each team member and foster an environment of mutual respect by listening well to others.

From a spiritual point of view, in a Christian-based organization, or when working with other Christians, a soul principle underlies a leader's commitment to listen well: the Holy Spirit speaks and works through every team member. One of the defining characteristics of the body of Christ is that the Spirit dwells inside each believer, enabling each one to make unique contributions that benefit the church, group, or team as a whole.[5] If we neglect any member's Spirit-enabled input, the whole body suffers. Thus, the more we value and trust the Holy Spirit's working in the lives of the whole team, the more we will listen for what the Spirit is saying through team members, and the more we will use their gifts for the benefit of the whole organization.

I'm not saying that every idea or point of view of an administrative assistant, junior executive, committee member, parishioner, or assistant pastor is going to contain wisdom or be Spirit-led, just as not all of our own ideas are always right on. I'm saying that the body of Christ assumes that God's Spirit works through every member of the team in ways that complement one another. Our job as leaders is to learn how to discern that divine activity and to listen for the voice of God amid all the other voices.

Over the years, I have discovered that listening to others has been hardest when I want to exert my leadership or when I am eager to get going and produce results. I'm sure I know the best way and want to get on with it. I may not have patience with others when they don't seem to understand or appreciate my point of view. Sometimes I assume they're not going to have much to offer, either because I have prejudged them or my history with them has lowered my expectations. At other times, I'm afraid that if I listen, I won't agree, and then I'll have a conflict to handle. Since I don't like conflict very much, either because it is too painful or too time-consuming, it seems easier not to ask if I don't want to know.

Listening to others can also be hard when we take personally the concerns others have expressed about our ideas. When we do that, we shift into a defensive mode that may produce a fight-or-flight response. Whether we attack or run for cover, we are not listening well, because we are not thoughtfully engaging with others to learn from them. When we feel the need to justify ourselves or our point of view more than to listen, all communication will eventually break down, as will the relationship.

Yes, there is a price to pay for taking the time to listen and solicit input from others. We often have to slow ourselves down against our will, to humble ourselves to listen when others challenge us in unkind and critical ways, to do more explaining and to hold more meetings than we want to, to adjust our agenda when others need to talk, or to extend timetables for projects. However, there is also a big price to pay for not listening. We are bound to lose wisdom, trust, and connection when we don't listen well and involve others in a respectful and open way. Ultimately we can undermine our ability to reach our goals. Often, it is pay now or pay later, with interest.

One of my painful memories of not listening well to others comes from my effort to make a specially written curriculum the basis for our evening youth programs. I had been pushing for staff not only to use the curriculum that the corporate office had spent many years and dollars writing, but to like it and appreciate it. When persuasion seemed unsuccessful with a handful of influential staff members, I tried to force change. While some new staff seemed to appreciate the curriculum, some of the old staff increasingly dug in their heels. They would use it, but they resented having to; they felt that I was not listening to their concerns. I kept thinking that we had resolved the issue, because I had laid down the law, but to my exasperation, murmurs and resistance kept surfacing.

However, when I finally slowed down and truly listened to their complaints without being defensive (I had been the overseer of the eight-year project and one of the editors), I was better able to absorb their comments. I learned that some of their concerns would also be mine: insufficient emphasis on biblical and spiritual issues; outdated activities; and preset topics that made youth leaders feel straitjacketed. When I took time to listen and showed a willingness to compromise, what resulted was a re-editing of the materials; more flexibility in when and how they were required to use it; and a better effort on my part to explain *why* the curriculum was important to our program. Simply put: the autocratic approach brought about compliance, but not cooperation, understanding, or improvement in effectiveness. Listening with an open heart and mind, with a willingness to be changed by what I learned from those most directly affected, led to a much better outcome—for the staff, for the youth, and for me as the leader.

Listening Pays Off

Sometimes when we hear a long list of actions we "should" do to be better leaders, we feel overwhelmed or discouraged. We may already feel weighted down with responsibilities. It may be that all the people who want us to listen to them are starting to confuse us. We may feel torn in many directions by a plethora of opinions with no resolution in sight. The conflict we feel between opposing viewpoints may be wearing us out.

Listen more? Ha! The only words that might be coming into our heads in response to all the voices resounding in our ears are "Shut up!"

At such low moments, we need to remember that the call to lead by listening well is intended to lighten our load, not to make it heavier. Developing and practicing good listening skills are not the same as giving up our authority to make decisions when necessary. In fact, listening can enhance our authority in the minds of those who follow, because while some people will respect us because of our official position of authority (our role on the organizational chart), most people will more eagerly confer authority on us when they genuinely respect us because of who we are and how we operate as leaders, and not because of our title. Then, as leaders, co-workers, and stakeholders learn to listen well to each other, everyone will garner more respect, goodwill, and loyalty from the others. Decisions will be better, commitment will be stronger, and tension will go down.

Conflict, on the other hand, may increase, because as a listening leader you have given permission to others to disagree with you and with one another, and to voice their differences. Yet we must remember that healthy conflict (respectful, honest, and unselfish expressions of differences in opinion by people devoted to the mission of the organization) is a good thing. As management consultant Patrick Lencioni explains, healthy conflict among team members who trust each other is essential to success:

> Teams that trust one another are not afraid to engage in passionate dialogue around issues and decisions that are key to the organization's success. They do not hesitate to disagree with, challenge, and question one another, all in the spirit of finding the best answers, discovering the truth, and making great decisions. . . . Teams that engage in unfiltered conflict are able to achieve genuine buy-in around important decisions, even when various members of the team initially disagree. That's because they ensure that all opinions and ideas are put on the table and considered, giving confidence to team members that no stone has been left unturned.[6]

Conflict, then, can be a sign of a healthy team, and is often necessary to reach good decisions. This dynamic is as true in the church and in other nonprofit organizations as it is in the secular world. Jonathan Rockford, executive director of Habitat for Humanity International, former executive of various Fortune 500 companies, and executive pastor of a large suburban church, said to me recently: "If there is trust, team members can engage in conflict safely and be willing to state contrary opinions." But not only will they feel safe to do so, they need to do so for the sake of the mission. That is, he stressed, organizations "need good conflict to get good decisions."

Indeed, conflict is to be welcomed, provided that there is mutual respect. "Iron sharpens iron, and one person sharpens the wits of another," one of the writers of Proverbs observes (Prov. 27:17 NRSV). However, we get into trouble as leaders when we allow conflict to degenerate into personal attacks or to undermine an appropriate decision-making process. If we give team members freedom to be disrespectful or rude to one another, malicious, or manipulative, open conflict will be hurtful and counterproductive. Likewise, if we allow the strongest or the most intimidating voice to make decisions for everyone else, we've let the team be hijacked. If, on the other hand, we are careful to establish the ground rules for expressing differences, by example or by explicit communication, we can create a safe and healthy environment.

We lead more effectively when we also identify where the ultimate decision-making authority lies, which varies depending on the situation (sometimes with the leader, sometimes with the majority, sometimes with a consensus, and sometimes with some other individual or body outside the group, such as a board of directors). We must not abdicate our position of leadership in the process of listening to others who think and feel differently, but that doesn't mean we have to go to either extreme of making all the decisions ourselves or of relinquishing control of the process to the most powerful individual or faction in the group. When we provide structural support to discussions by clearly delineating process and authority, we can encourage full and energetic participation on the part of everyone, and still bring the matter to a close when we think it best to do so.

Listening well to and drawing fully on the team still require the leader to determine how and when a decision will be made. How a leader includes the team in the final decision depends on what kind of team is involved. In football, the quarterback or coach decides what play to run. On the battlefield, the commander makes the final decision. On the U.S. Supreme Court, the justices vote, and the majority rules. Further, even when the group members think that the group is making a decision together, there is usually a prime influencer in every group who decides for the group, whether appointed or elected or not. So-called group consensus is often reached after strong or influential individuals voice their opinions and others resonate with it or acquiesce to it. If someone else came along with an equally persuasive appeal or who held esteem in their eyes, many on the team would switch their positions instantly.

As spiritual leaders in a faith-based setting, our listening communicates that we expect the Holy Spirit to work through each member of the team and organization in various valuable ways. Listening expresses that we value what comes from the Spirit more than getting our own way, having to be right, exerting our power, or anything else that would exalt us and our agenda at the expense of the mission and the team.

In a secular setting, spiritual leadership means expecting God to work in us and through us to communicate God's love to others. We will listen to others, regardless of the nature of their spiritual life, to show respect and to benefit from their insights and point of view. On a deeper level, we can also listen for the truth God may choose to reveal through our listening to others. We may learn something about ourselves, our methods of leading, the impact our policies have on others, how nonbelievers experience us, and so forth.

As staff members come to believe that we genuinely value them and their gifts—and, in a Christian setting, that we are expecting the Holy Spirit to speak through them—they will more likely want to work with us instead of against us. They will more likely want to cooperate with us and one another than to compete or oppose. As studies have shown, most people value being able to contribute in meaningful ways and being appreciated, above other rewards such as a higher salary and more vacation time. People want to be a valued part of a team whose members are loyal to each other more than they want to be in a dog-eat-dog environment in which they always have to watch their back and look over their shoulder. Our respectful, affirming inclusion of others by listening well elicits the cooperation, active engagement, and loyalty we all desire.

Here's Help

Leading by listening well can take different forms. In strategic planning, for example, taking time to listen to representatives from every group affected by possible change or lack of change will greatly enrich the information-gathering process. When an entire organization is concerned, written surveys, area reports, or focus groups can provide valuable information that can be shared with the leaders. For smaller issues, such as those related to single departments or work teams, leaders may have the time to listen on a one-to-one basis and to attend team meetings.

Regardless of setting, constituency, and scope of issue, what's most important is to develop a leadership style characterized by some specific listening practices. Gaining greater self-awareness about our strengths and weaknesses as a listener will be helpful as well. To this end, the triad exercise at the end of this section may be a helpful tool for you, your leadership team, and others within your organization.

Listening Practices

Each of the following three practices is essential for creating a good listening environment. Each draws on material already presented in this chapter. Leaders need to take responsibility to put these practices in place in a group or organization. Yet often, the best leaders will invite co-workers, staff members, and other team members to participate in creating the process and a positive environment for teamwork. The leader must decide who participates on work teams and what sharing leadership means in each situation, while those who are not designated as leaders have an important role to work with the leaders toward agreed-upon goals.

Create an atmosphere of trust and safety

Others will be most likely to talk constructively if you, as the leader, have created and maintained a standard for respectful communication. This includes the following:

1. No punishment (or backlash) for earnest opinions expressed appropriately.
2. Stay open as much as possible throughout a decision-making process.[7] If we are not truly open to the input of others, our "listening" is a charade and lacks integrity.

We maintain our integrity by not entering a process when the outcome is a foregone conclusion. We prove our openness by being willing to change our viewpoints, modify our expectations or approach, change plans altogether, or otherwise compromise when it is in the best interests of the goals of the organization.

3. Demonstrate that you are genuinely listening and value the input of others. Use reflective listening skills as one way to demonstrate that you have truly heard what others are saying.[8] Encourage group members to use good listening skills with one another.[9]

Create and work a process to listen and decide

1. Clearly identify the problem, challenge, or need, as you see it. Invite team members to help with naming and narrowing the focus of the group's task.
2. Clarify how a decision will be made, when, and by whom; include the scope of responsibility of the group (to do fact finding, to make recommendations, or to make a decision), and identify what individual or group has the final authority to make whatever decisions will need to be made.
3. Invite input from others; encourage discussion, including disagreement.[10]
4. Encourage prayer and listening for God to speak to us through one another.[11]
5. Work for consensus as much as possible, but do not be afraid to make a decision when it is in the best interests of the organization and possibly the team to do so. (For example, sometimes timeliness is an issue, and action is needed. At other times, the group members just don't have the wisdom or the will to come up with a good course of action. In such cases, it helps for one of the group members who is able to do so to put a working plan on the table to elicit thoughts and reactions. Then, when it appears to the leader that no more useful input will be forthcoming or that group participation is

reaching the point of diminishing returns, it is best either to bring discussion to a close for the day, or to bring the process to a close and announce a decision.)

6. Bring closure to the process by signaling when gathering input or discussion is finished, which should come as no surprise to anyone if you have done a good job with steps 2 and 3. Then make a clear decision that everyone understands, and implement the decision as soon as possible.

Bringing closure to the process and then acting on the decision made are important to keep faith with those who participated with the expectation of achieving tangible results. If we perpetuate our "listening" too long, the process can become counterproductive, demoralizing participants and delaying needed action. Sometimes we don't bring closure under the guise of listening—sometimes we are actually taking a passive role, avoiding conflict, or becoming mired in indecision. Group processes need to have a clear goal, a workable process, full and constructive participation, and closure.

Be careful not to overreact or react prematurely

1. Beware of reacting verbally or nonverbally to others' thoughts and feelings, especially if you are feeling defensive or embarrassed, or otherwise take the viewpoint personally.

2. Counterproductive reactions may include rolling your eyes, sighing, furrowing your brows, adding an edge to your voice, and giving other physical indicators of displeasure.

   For some, reacting strongly may be cathartic or even fun, but remember that you are in a position of leadership and that people will hear more than your thoughts and feelings when you communicate. They will hear what you say as "the opinion of the boss"—a fact that can make them uncomfortable about disagreeing with you or worried about upsetting you. They may also give too much weight to your opinion, and be excessively hurt by your disapproval.

Thus, if we value the input of others, we must be careful not to inhibit a free flow of convictions and opinions, especially by rebuking, overpowering, or appearing to manipulate those who have the courage to speak up. Remember, we *want* others to participate freely as long as they are on task.

3. However, if someone's participation is clearly counterproductive or off task, you may need to redirect the conversation. Sometimes others will try to sabotage a process, work out their anger or resentment of others, or in some other way reflect a relational breakdown by negative comments or behavior in a group meeting. We need wisdom and discretion in handling each situation constructively. Sometimes the person needs a gentle reminder of norms for group discussion, sometimes a sharp verbal kick in the pants is in order, and sometimes we need to stop the process altogether to attend to the relational issues that are suddenly exposed for all to see. At other times, we may need to be patient, because some may need time to figure out what they think and feel, especially if they are fearful. In such cases, these individuals may appear to be off task or reacting counterproductively when they are really figuring out what they want to say.

Reflection Questions

After reading this chapter, write your response to the reflection questions below in the space provided, on three-by-five-inch cards, or in your own journal. Invite staff members, a leadership team, or a group of professional peers to meet together to work through these questions in triads as well. Dialogues and triads would be especially relevant for leaders who want to gain more insight into their own listening skills and to promote listening well within the corporate culture. (See the "Here's Help" section of chapter 1 for more detailed instructions on how to conduct triads and additional comments on this exercise.)

1. What troubling tensions exist because of lack of either communication or mutual understanding between my co-workers or staff and me?

2. What do I need to learn to become a more effective listener?

3. What message has my organization or co-workers been trying to get me to hear that I dare not ignore any longer?

Instructions for Triads (10 minutes)

Four minutes: Speaker shares with listener his or her responses to the reflection questions. Observer keeps time and pays attention to nonverbal communication.

Four minutes: Listener helps speaker process thoughts and experiences by asking clarifying questions. Listener's role is not to introduce his or her own opinions or to pry, but to ask for further clarification of ideas and feelings speaker has shared. Observer keeps time and notices any dynamics that emerge during the give-and-take between speaker and listener.

Two minutes: Observer shares what he or she has seen, heard, thought, wondered about, or felt while observing speaker and listener.

Switch roles and repeat the process until each person has had the opportunity to be in each role.

Reflection on the Exercise

Take a minute to jot down a reflection on your experience(s) in the triad exercise. Then compare notes with others in your group. What struck you as significant?

* As speaker . . .

* As listener . . .

* As observer . . .

Finish the exercise by sharing with each other one thing you heard expressed by others that you want to think and pray carefully about in the coming week.

Something to Think About

For fun, if you find that you resist committing yourself to being a listening leader, it may help to remember Balaam's ass (Num. 22:21-35). If God can speak through a donkey, he can speak even through the youth pastor, the cafeteria attendant, the bus driver, the chair of the board, the middle-schooler whose hair is covering his eyes so that you're not sure who's talking to you, or anyone else who happens to have your e-mail address. I'm speaking tongue in cheek, of course, but effective leaders do maintain a certain level of humility about their own limitations, along with high sense of expectation about what God can reveal and do in mysterious ways.

TRUSTING GOD

Leadership Practice
Always trust God.

Soul Principle
Steadfast trust in God is indispensable to
spiritual vitality and leadership.

I didn't trust God anymore.

Ten years of one disillusioning, disappointing, heart-wrenching experience after another had shaken my faith. Oh, I still worshiped and believed in Christ, but something had shifted inside me. And the changes weren't all good.

I chose not to teach during the 1995 January term at Hamline University, so that I could attend an eight-day spiritual retreat, "Healing for the Nations," in Colorado Springs. We worshiped, we prayed, and we did some soul-searching and exploring of childhood issues and self-image. I was looking for some guidance from God about my future. I was completely surprised by what I received.

The second night I suddenly realized that something was wrong with my relationship with God. I didn't know how long I had felt this way, but unexpectedly the truth was right before me. I felt I had honored God with my life and life's work, and, from my perspective, God had let me down. Though I was at the retreat still looking to God to help me, I abruptly realized that, at the core of my being, I didn't really trust God anymore. There had been too much disappointment and pain, and I blamed God.

In the mid-1980s, my wife and I served as pastors of a small congregation outside Chicago. During our four years there, we lost one child in a miscarriage, and my roommate from college died at the age of 28. Our church chugged along, but I soon discovered that even though I was working up to 70 hours a week, my effort wasn't going to be enough. While meaningful ministry was taking place, forces much larger than I were keeping this congregation from becoming the growing, vibrant ministry I had envisioned. I didn't know why God didn't seem to be helping more.

Then I got sick. On June 24, 1986, the day after my first son was born, my dermatologist's grave tone on the telephone alerted me to trouble. He tried to break it to me gently. I had been diagnosed with a fatal skin disease. I had perhaps 10 good years left, he told me.

Hearing this prognosis was like being socked in the gut. What was going on? God had not blessed our efforts at the church the way I had expected. He didn't save our daughter from death, and now it looked as though my newborn son was going to be fatherless before becoming a teenager, and my wife a widow.

Then my mother got Alzheimer's disease. In 1988, we knew something was wrong. By the early 1990s, her diagnosis was confirmed, and her condition continued to worsen. My father was forced to retire early. All their plans for their retirement years disintegrated. We watched helplessly as his health declined faster than hers. There was little we could do to help either of them. As it turned out, the stress of caring for her took my father's life in 1998, long before she eventually died in 2002.

None of this made sense to me. Both of my parents had been faithful and devoted workers at a Christian college, and yet God didn't seem to take care of them. I had worked as hard as I knew how in Christian ministry, and instead of being blessed, I was surrounded by sickness and death. I didn't realize it at the time, but I had entered into full-time Christian ministry with an implicit contract with God: I would serve faithfully, and the Lord would take care of me.

Now, I don't know what I thought "take care of" actually meant. In retrospect, I suppose I unconsciously assumed that my family and I would be protected from harm and that God would bless me with a fruitful ministry to some undefined extent. Whatever I expected, though, I knew I wasn't getting it. All the pain, losses, disappointment, and struggles without more "to show for" my hard work and faithfulness just didn't seem right. God had failed my parents, my family, my church, and me, so I thought, and my disappointment had begun to turn to doubt and bitterness.

I was at a crossroads, and I knew it. I realized that to go forward, I was going to have to decide: was I going to choose to trust God or not? I could no longer serve as a Christian leader and teacher while secretly doubting God's goodness and activity in my life. I had seen the problem, and now I was going to have to choose: continue to be bitter about my mother's disease and all the other losses in my life, or choose to trust that God was somehow still active in my life for good in ways that I could not fully understand or discern.

If I could have proved that God was active in the midst of my sorrow and difficulties, or could have proved that God wasn't, then I wouldn't have had to choose either doubt and bitterness or trust. However, I had no such proof. On one hand, I had my many painful experiences, and on the other I had to admit that I had matured and gained many insights into life and leadership through my trials. Moreover, we had developed meaningful relationships with parishioners who seemed to have been helped significantly by our ministry. Thus, in the absence of clear "proof" one way or another, I realized that trusting in God was going to be a choice, not a conclusion based on incontrovertible facts.

Logically, there was a third option. I could have chosen to jettison my belief in God altogether, neither trusting that God is loving and good nor remaining bitter at a God who seemingly might not be good or care about me. However, the truth was, I *did* believe in God. I was sure of my salvation. Despite my doubt and bitterness, God had blessed me with increased faith and appreciation for God's grace and for Jesus Christ. I also had experienced the love of God in ways that had brought me much comfort, joy, and peace. It would have been thoroughly dishonest for me to pretend that I no longer believed in God or for me to claim that God wasn't loving—there was too much in my heart, mind, and experience that suggested otherwise. Yet, at the same time, it would have been just as dishonest if I did not own up to the huge block that was hindering my relationship with God. The truth was, I had a trust problem.

When all this became clear to me, I knew in an instant what I would choose. I was sick of carrying around bitterness in my heart, and I was eager to resolve the cognitive dissonance I had been experiencing. Instead of blaming God for my difficult life experiences, I could trust in the God of the Bible, whom I loved and had come to know in many meaningful ways over the years.

Trust was a choice in the midst of ambiguous circumstances. It was faith in the unseen rather than a logical conclusion based on hard evidence. In a moment that felt like the equivalent of scales falling from my eyes, I could suddenly see what I had been blind to. I realized I could choose to trust God, and I grabbed the option—gladly.

God had given me the grace I needed to put my trust in him, and that experience became another turning point in my life. It felt like a healing and a fresh start. Later on in the week, while in prayer, I saw a mental image of myself walking side by side with Jesus as I went forward in ministry. For the first time in many years, I didn't feel alone anymore.

What's Needed

Always trust God.

Our world needs more leaders who have experienced the transforming power of God to set them free from doubt, fear, insecurity, an overdependence on logic and proof, and any other hindrance that keeps them from a life- and leadership-changing faith. Churches, companies, and organizations need leaders who love Christ from their hearts and understand what it means to live and lead by faith. They need leaders who, by the grace of God, stand at the crossroads of doubt and faith and consistently choose to trust God with their life, their family, their leadership.

I'm not talking about living in denial or in an idealized spiritual state of existence that hardly anyone could ever reach. I'm describing fallible, less-than-whole leaders—because that's the only kind there are—who have nonetheless faced their own demons and are actively working through their faith issues. They have admitted their disappointment, frustration, anger, and even bitterness, but they refuse to remain stuck. They are seeking to let the light of faith shine on their darkest thoughts, fears, pain, and distress, so that they may consistently live and lead from a place of genuine trust in God. Rather than letting their troubles turn them inward or undermine their confidence, vitality, or ability to lead, they will choose to believe that God has not abandoned them and will look for God's activity in the midst of their life and leadership.

Faith's Perspective

Faith is "being sure of what we hope for and certain of what we do not see" (Heb. 11:1). Faith does not dictate to God what the results of our work must be, but trusts that God is producing valuable outcomes in one way or another. Faith trusts that God is at work in our life and leadership whether or not we can discern his activity. Faith does not rely on magical answers or even miracles. Faith eagerly looks to God to work for good in all situations, but on God's terms, not necessarily ours (Rom. 8:28-29).

Faith trusts that God truly is compassionate, gracious, slow to anger, abounding in love and faithfulness (Exod. 34:6). Faith refuses to jump to the false conclusion that our painful experiences demonstrate that God doesn't care or isn't involved in human affairs. Faith clings to God, even if all our hopes, dreams, loved ones, and life itself perish. Faith does not glibly call our painful disappointments, tragedies, and suffering "good." Rather, it acknowledges the horror in the human condition but looks to the one source of hope that remains when all else fades away.

Ultimately, faith surrenders all claims on "expected outcomes" in this life. It looks beyond the present to eternity, trusting that nothing can separate believers from the love of God and that God will never leave us nor forsake us (Rom. 8:35-39; Heb. 13:5).

Long-term Faith for Short-term Issues

There's one scene in the movie *Titanic* that I think of often. The ship is sinking, and the priest is reading Scripture and offering solace to those who are about to die. Now, I'm quite sure that many of those huddled around him were seeking a miraculous rescue. That's human nature, and perfectly understandable and appropriate. Scripture encourages us to call out to God for help when we are in trouble.

I wonder, however, what the priest was thinking when he read Psalm 23 to the desperate crowd. Was he reading Scripture as a magical incantation to invoke God's help? Was he naïvely expecting God to produce special help for the believers, or maybe even for everyone—an outcome that we know in retrospect did not materialize for the vast majority? Or did he know what many seasoned pastors and spiritual leaders have learned: faith in God does not guarantee health, safety, help, or blessing—though these things often are provided. Faith in God in the midst of crisis is ultimately about clinging to the only source of long-term hope for our lives. Of course, it is natural to wish for happy circumstances in the short run. But a mature perspective recognizes that what matters the most is the long run—our eternal destiny in relationship with God, and how God intends to work in our present circumstances for eternal purposes.

A good friend of mine was diagnosed with cancer that had metastasized to the bone. Panic and distress were evident in his and his wife's faces and voices when I first sat down to talk with them about their unexpected news. Part of them was in shock and disbelief. Another part of them began bargaining with God, and pleading for a miracle. They attempted to conjure up as much faith as possible, assuming that the more faith they had, the more God could or would help them. They were desperate. Every reaction was completely normal and understandable. They needed their friends to gather around them to help them maintain faith and keep from collapsing under the weight of the terror, and to encourage him to fight the cancer.

My heart broke for them and for their children. Yet even more, I longed for them to have the kind of long-term faith that looked beyond the immediate crisis and their desperate clinging to their notion of what *had* to happen—healing. I prayed for his cure and prayed that they would be able to sense God's love and presence in the midst of this ordeal. I also prayed for an ability to take comfort in their eternal hope, and to see the good God wanted to do amid their suffering.

Whether my friend beat the cancer or not, they needed a faith that could propel them into a more intimate relationship with God and into a mode of living that made the most of every opportunity the illness would produce. Then, if he was not going to live, they would need a strong, long-term faith to get them through all that lay ahead, especially the wife, who would be left behind with several children still at home. She needed to believe that she could make it without him, as sad and difficult as that would be. She would need a long-term perspective that took hope, comfort, and purpose from her eternal relationship with God, come what may along the path of this life.

As a leader, how will you react when answers aren't forthcoming, conflict arises, solutions don't magically appear, vision is uncertain, the staff members you cherish leave and the ineffective ones stay, the money doesn't come in, you don't see the fruit you worked so hard for, and prayers don't seem to be answered? What will you do? Do you have a long-term faith as a foundation to handle the short-term issues?

Choosing to trust, no matter what, is not an abdication of our leadership responsibility to get to the bottom of whatever problem has emerged and to work out solutions. When a crisis erupts, the best course of action is often to address it as soon as possible. Truly, we are not to look to God instead of doing our job. Rather, we are to keep a long-term faith perspective in the midst of fulfilling our responsibilities. Trust is continuing to believe that God is present and at work in our organization, even if we cannot discern how at the moment. As spiritual leaders committed to trusting God always, we continue to work faithfully, to seek wisdom, and to make whatever hard decisions are needed. But we also continue to rest in the unbreakable bond of our love relationship with God and in God's sovereign activity to accomplish his good, pleasing, and acceptable will (Rom. 12:2).

What's Real

Steadfast trust in God is indispensable to
spiritual vitality and leadership.

Let's face it. It simply does not work to try to patch trust on top of unresolved negative feelings and nagging doubt. Our own sense of integrity and our ability to lead others in convincing and authentic ways demand that our faith be real. Our trust has to go deeper than quoting Bible verses or trying to put a good face on a bad situation. Otherwise, our spiritual leadership will be hollow.

Throughout my dark days of doubt and loss of trust, thanks to the grace of God, I kept experiencing moments of blessing and encouragement. But I could tell in my preaching, teaching, and counseling that sometimes I just didn't have the heart to tell others truly to put their faith in God. (Conversely, at times I think I preached faith really hard, perhaps because I was trying to convince myself.) Then, when crises came, I found it easy to doubt God's presence and care.

As a result, I found myself drifting from a ministry of proclamation of the gospel and promotion of faith and gravitating toward ministries of compassion and service. My heart genuinely went out to those who were suffering. Perhaps I wanted to make up for what I perceived to be God's abandonment of hurting people. I don't know. I wanted to do something concrete with my life that offered a sure hope to others in this present life that didn't depend so much on faith in an unseen God and an unknown future. I figured that by doing acts of service, I would, at the end of my life, have something to show for myself, something I could feel good about.

I could do social service from a caring heart. I could teach New Testament from an academic point of view. I could discuss theological subjects intellectually. But ask me to lead the charge as a leader among Christians, living and serving by faith, and something would have been missing—not heart, not mind, but soul.

Pastors, executives, and administrators must be grounded in genuine faith to be effective spiritual leaders. Those who continue to trust in God, come what may, experience personal strength and stability that enables them to stand strong and to help others who are suffering distress and uncertainty. Jeremiah expresses the spiritual principle this way: "Blessed are those who trust in the LORD, whose trust is the LORD. They shall be like a tree planted by water, sending out its roots by the stream. It shall not fear when heat comes, and its leaves shall stay green; in the year of drought it is not anxious, and it does not cease to bear fruit" (Jer. 17:7-8 NRSV).

Ultimately, to develop this kind of genuine faith depends on God's work of transformation within us. All of us need help to be the spiritually authentic and mature leaders that the world is crying out for. We can set out to trust as an act of the will, but we will not get where we need to be without God to transform our hearts and minds along the way. Our part is to draw on whatever resources are available to us. We can turn to pastors, counselors, spiritually mature friends, teachers, books, seminars, long walks, spiritual disciplines, therapeutic retreats, and other helpful tools to seek God and God's work of transformation within us. Our prayer is that God will bless us with eyes to see the ways he is at work in our lives and leadership, and will create within us a steadfast faith, with a long-term perspective.

Here's Help

Trusting in God is certainly not a new idea for most of us. The call to put our trust in God is at the core of biblical teaching and the Judeo-Christian tradition. The Psalmist wrote, "[W]hen I am afraid, I put my trust in you. In God, whose word I praise, in God I trust; I am not afraid; what can flesh do to me?" (Ps. 56:3-4 NRSV). When Jesus was about to be arrested and led to his death, he urged his disciples to continue to rely on God and on him. He said, "Do not let your hearts be troubled. Trust in God; trust also in me" (John 14:1 NIV). Even the United States currency declares, "In God we trust."

Yet, in the practical world of living and leading, I have struggled to know what exactly I am to trust God for, apart from my eternal salvation. Is there anything I can count on God for in the short term? Or are the only solid promises for the long term? What can I, as an individual, as a leader, as a member of a church or group, expect from God? If God is faithful, what does that mean in practical terms?

What follows is a series of guidelines and appropriate expectations for the person of faith, based on the teaching of Scripture. None provides a prescription for specific action in any given situation. Rather, they provide the theological foundation for maintaining an attitude of trust in God, from which you can offer strong, solid leadership.

Remember your limited ability to understand the will and ways of God.

> For my thoughts are not your thoughts, neither are your ways my ways, says the LORD. For as the heavens are higher than the earth, so are my ways higher than your ways, and my thoughts than your thoughts.
>
> Isaiah 55:8-9 NIV

After Jesus' death, two disciples met Jesus on the road to Emmaus. When he asked them what they were discussing, "they stood still, looking sad" (Luke 24:17 NRSV).

Beware of getting "stuck" on the road of life, stopped in your tracks with downcast faces, supposing all is lost. When life's events just don't make sense to you and you cannot imagine how God could be a part of what is happening, remember the limitations of your ability to grasp the ways of the Lord. God may be up to something that you cannot even imagine, let alone comprehend.

Expect God to be at work in your life and leadership, leading and guiding you.

> Trust in the LORD with all your heart and lean not on your own understanding; in all your ways acknowledge him, and he will make your paths straight.
>
> Proverbs 3:5-6 NIV

> If any of you is lacking in wisdom, ask God, who gives to all generously and ungrudgingly, and it will be given you. But ask in faith, never doubting, for the one who doubts is like a wave of the sea, driven and tossed by the wind.
>
> James 1:5-6 NRSV

Trusting in God, honoring God and God's will in decision making, and asking for wisdom—none of these actions guarantees that we will automatically know the will of God or discern the best course of action in every situation. Nor am I suggesting that we are called to trust that every decision we make is inspired by God just because we pray or seek to submit our will to God's. In fact, some of us may have tried praying for wisdom, only to make the worst possible decision. Wise individuals and effective leaders know that they often need to draw on a whole host of resources, experts, and experiences to make good decisions.

Nevertheless, spiritually mature individuals and leaders know also the tremendous value of seeking God's leading and guidance in little and big ways, every day, in every aspect of their life. Each of us has to learn how to discern God's activity in our life over time. But faith believes that God is active and wants us to submit our will to his, not to jump to conclusions based on our own understanding of circumstances; to seek Spirit-inspired wisdom and direction, and to trust that in various ways, the Lord will direct our paths, according to his will.

Expect God to build character and faith out of your experiences of suffering.

> We also rejoice in our sufferings, because we know that suffering produces perseverance; perseverance, character; and character, hope. And hope does not disappoint us, because God has poured out his love into our hearts by the Holy Spirit, whom he has given us.
>
> Romans 5:3-5 NIV

> We know that all things work together for good for those who love God, who are called according to his purpose. For those whom he foreknew he also predestined to be conformed to the image of his Son, in order that he might be the firstborn within a large family.
>
> Romans 8:28-29 NRSV

In this [hope of salvation] you greatly rejoice, though now for a little while you may have had to suffer grief in all kinds of trials. These have come so that your faith—of greater worth than gold, which perishes even though refined by fire—may be proved genuine and may result in praise, glory and honor when Jesus Christ is revealed. Though you have not seen him, you love him; and even though you do not see him now, you believe in him and are filled with an inexpressible and glorious joy for you are receiving the goal of your faith, the salvation of your souls.

1 Peter 1:6-9 NIV

Some Christians become bitter when they go through tragedy, such as the loss of a child, a horrible accident, or a brutal crime. They may feel abandoned. They can't imagine a good God allowing such a thing, and certainly can't see any good in it. The first thing to remember in such circumstances is that God's actions in history (in Christ's life, sacrificial death, and resurrection, and in many aspects of our life experience) encourage us to believe that God will continue to work in our life for good, ultimately bringing us salvation from judgment and death.

Second, in the Romans passages, Paul did not say that God caused our suffering. We simply do not know when God's hand is behind a human event. Instead, the assurance of these passages is that, regardless of what happens, all things work together for good in the Christian's life. Regardless of the source of our trials, God is at work transforming our painful ordeals into constructive outcomes, which God defines as our becoming more and more like Christ.

Third, Paul doesn't say that we will always be able to discern the good at the time, or perhaps even in this life. However, as our minds become renewed and as we experience transformation, we will be increasingly able to discern that God's will is good (Rom. 12:2).

Fourth, the good Paul had in mind in Romans 8 is our becoming more and more like Christ—that and experiencing our salvation. He does not promise a long, happy, and prosperous life according to our agenda. While humans tend to focus on this life and define good only in temporal terms, God's perspective is eternal. We tend to care about life, liberty, and the pursuit of happiness. God cares about character, an enduring relationship with him, and our bringing glory and honor to him.

In 1 Peter 1, we read that our hope for the long term provides a foundation for hope and joy in the short term. Regardless of the source of any given trial, God's purposes in our suffering include demonstrating to us and others that God has truly created a solid faith within us. However, God's ultimate goal in using suffering so that our faith may be "proved genuine and may result in praise, glory and honor when Jesus Christ is revealed" (1 Pet. 1:7) is achieved through a process that often reveals our weakness before it establishes our strength.

Here's how the process often works. When times get tough, our level of spiritual, emotional, and psychological maturity is exposed. When we are immature in our faith, trials may reveal our readiness to run for cover, doubt, rebel, or give up. However, once we get past our initial reaction and look again to God to work in our situation for good, we perceive and experience the good, and our faith is refined and strengthened.

Over time, then, our experience of turning to God in times of trial teaches us that our hope is in God alone, and we learn to respond more readily in faith in the midst of suffering. We learn to lift our eyes off our present circumstances and to focus increasingly on God and God's promises for our ultimate salvation. As our faith is strengthened and shown to be increasingly solid, Christ will receive praise, glory, and honor, because others will see that the transformation that has taken place in our life is rooted in Christ and in our faith in him.

Despite the gloomy medical prognosis I received in 1986, my skin disease is completely healed. To be sure, my family and I are thrilled. Yet even more, the ordeal that thrust us into fear, uncertainty, self-examination, and dependence on God has been spiritually transformative for us. I would wish this experience on no one, but I would pray that everyone may have opportunities to learn how God brings good out of such trauma and to experience God's blessings amid sufferings.

Take encouragement from opportunities to share in the sufferings of Christ.

> Now if we are children, then we are heirs—heirs of God and co-heirs with Christ, if indeed we share in his sufferings in order that we may also share in his glory.
>
> Romans 8:17 NIV

Apart from the suffering that we experience from trials and loss, sometimes suffering comes as a direct result of serving Christ. In many places in the world, Christians suffer physically for their faith. Others experience psychological and emotional suffering, too. At the very least, Christians should expect an unbelieving world to react in ways similar to the people of Jesus' time: with disbelief, false accusation, anger, hatred, jealousy, rejection, and opposition. While painful and often stressful, sharing in the suffering of Christ has been considered a privilege by Christians in every generation.

Cling to Jesus Christ, who will never let you go.

> "Never will I leave you, never will I forsake you," says the Lord.
>
> Hebrews 13:5 NIV

> For I am convinced that neither death nor life, neither angels nor demons, neither the present nor the future, nor any powers, neither height nor depth, nor anything else in all creation, will be able to separate us from the love of God that is in Christ Jesus our Lord.
>
> Romans 8:38-39 NIV

There's one ill-advised comment I periodically hear Christian leaders make when something good happens in their organization or ministry: "God showed up." They got the contribution they were hoping for, so "God showed up." They got the contract, they met their goals, they came to a consensus, so "God showed up." They probably mean to say that God's presence became evident in tangible ways or that they experienced the Holy Spirit in a special way. However, if those who say such things are intending to give God credit for something, such language could backfire for a person who is suffering and doesn't happen to see or feel God's presence at a given moment. It's bad theology to think that God is present only when things go our way.

Mature spiritual leaders will not base their belief in the presence or absence of God on whether they get the results they wanted. They will trust not only that God always shows up, but also that God never leaves. God is always present, whether we perceive his presence or not. As we cling to our faith in Jesus, we may be assured that God will continue to love us and to keep our souls safe in his care for eternity.

The Lord's love and presence with us does not guarantee freedom from suffering and death, but he assures us that he will not abandon us, no matter what we may have to face. Whatever painful experiences we endure are simply not the final word in our lives. Trust means believing that, all appearances to the contrary notwithstanding, God is still for us, and that nothing can sever the eternal bond of love between us. God is continually acting to accomplish his good, pleasing, and perfect will, even in times that we must pass through the valley of the shadow of death on the way. "'Never will I leave you, never will I forsake you,' says the Lord" (Heb. 13:5 NIV).

Something to Think About

Why are you downcast, O my soul? Why so disturbed within me? Put your hope in God, for I will yet praise him, my Savior and my God.

Psalm 42:5-6a NRSV

Many things can go "wrong" in life and leadership. Sometimes our experience is incredibly painful, as when someone betrays us or dies. But the degree of the pain or the difficulty of the challenge does not invalidate the basic biblical truth: our suffering provides an opportunity for us to grow and to see God work in surprising ways for good, by his definition.

When things go well, we may hardly think about faith in God. But when things turn sour or overwhelm us, trust becomes a huge issue. Each experience is a fork in the road. The way we respond will make all the difference in the world. The more we choose to trust, the more we will stay attuned to the good that God is producing through our circumstances, and to our opportunity to be part of God's activity—consciously, fruitfully, and joyfully.

In your journal or in the space provided below, and later with a trusted friend or your leadership team, reflect on the following questions. Ask yourself:

- What issue do I need to resolve with God emotionally so that I can get back on track with living and leading from a place of trust?

- Where will I go for help to work through my faith issues?

- What teaching of Scripture do I need to remember and cling to in my darkest moments of doubt, fear, or suffering?

- What language do my leadership team and I need to adopt to communicate more clearly our faith and commitment always to trust God?

THE HEART
OF SPIRITUAL LEADERSHIP

Leadership Practice
Open yourself fully to the love and grace of God.

Soul Principle
The grace of God creates the only sure foundation for
personal transformation and dynamic spiritual leadership.

Of all the things I have learned and experienced as a Christian
and as a leader, the greatest learning by far has come from
experiencing the immensity of God's love and the life-changing power of God's grace.

By the gracious provision of God, I arrived in Minneapolis
with my family in 1993, just in time for a weeklong seminar
on shame conducted by therapist and author Jeff
VanVonderen.[1] Since I was unemployed, I was free to attend.
What I heard that first night has changed my life forever. Jeff
talked about the prevalence of shame in our culture. Many
psychologists differentiate between shame and guilt. Guilt is

feeling bad about something you've done, while shame is feeling bad about yourself as a person—that is, you have not only done something bad; you *are* bad. He explained that when shame is in the soil of our lives, it produces a variety of fruit or plants. One is like a weed, which we would all recognize readily: negative, self-defeating, self-destructive behavior. At core, the people whose lives "grow weeds" have a low self-image and fail to see the good that God is doing in their lives. We see the symptoms all the time in the culture around us: kids and adults taking drugs, eating or drinking excessively, engaging in casual sex, cutting themselves, even attempting suicide. I thought, yes, that makes sense.

But I wasn't prepared for what Jeff said next. He explained that another kind of plant that grows from soil contaminated by shame may actually look beautiful. It is the flower of high achievement. The people who cultivate this flower work hard to prove to themselves and to others that they really are OK. Now, achievement can be a very good thing, but not when we are driven to perform and to achieve as a desperate attempt to feel good about ourselves. At some point, we may give up out of frustration and discouragement. Or we may keep pushing and driving ourselves to exhaustion without finding the peace we seek.

The message pierced my heart. With a bachelor's degree and three graduate degrees, I knew I was driven, at least in part, to seek my self-worth in my accomplishments. But as I sat in the audience, unemployed, smarting from years of searching unsuccessfully for the right job and from frequent rejection, I felt like a failure. I didn't feel very valuable as a person. I couldn't have even articulated how bad I felt about myself at the time, but I realize now that I was filled with shame—shame over past sin, shame over inadequacy and missteps, shame over rejection, shame over not having a job. All my failures and shortcomings started piling up on each other. On top of that, my wife's family was full of successful business people. Later that night I was supposed to go to a family party where I would hear about their accomplishments and positions of power and influence. All I could imagine that I could offer in response to their polite inquiries would be, "No, I *still* don't have a job."

By now, I was hanging on every word Jeff said. He explained that there is a better way to live life and to view myself. Instead of looking to my abilities or achievements to feel good about myself, I could look to God and God's view of me. I am loved because I am a precious creation of God, not because of my accomplishments, status, or popularity. And, yes, sin is a problem, but God has taken care of that, too. That was the purpose of Jesus' life and death. That's how great God's love for us is: "[W]hile we still were sinners, Christ died for us" (Rom. 5:8 NRSV). God loves me as one of his own and has forgiven me for all of my sins.

That night I realized that while I still needed a job, what I truly needed was a sense of assurance about my worth and value in God's eyes. I needed to let go of all my striving, my attempts to feel good about myself on the basis of my own performance, and to rest in God's love, mercy, and grace.

What's Needed

Open yourself fully to the love and grace of God.

A pervasive sense of shame, sometimes called toxic shame, creates a negative self-image that eats away at our sense of lovability and value. We believe that something is irredeemably wrong with us, and we consciously or unconsciously carry a sense of deficiency that affects every aspect of our lives. Some of us deal with our shame by denial—we try to persuade ourselves that we don't have a problem; everyone else does. Some of us try to medicate our pain through drugs, excessive use of alcohol, workaholism, sex, constant activity, and a host of other distracting or temporarily comforting activities. As was true of me, many seek comfort from trying to achieve or impress others. However, the only lasting cure for shame, whatever the symptoms in a person's life, is the love and grace of God.

The Protestant tradition has done a particularly good job of highlighting our need to trust in God's action on our behalf, independent of our own efforts. As the apostle Paul clearly taught:

> For by grace you have been saved through faith, and this is not your own doing; it is the gift of God—not the result of works, so that no one may boast.
>
> Ephesians 2:8-9 NRSV

What is truly life-transforming, though, is *experiencing* the love and grace of God in a personal way. The Bible is full of stories about men and women whose lives were changed because of their encounter with God the Father, the Lord Jesus Christ, or the Holy Spirit. While the narratives of Scripture are descriptive, not prescriptive (that is, they don't tell us exactly how you and I are to experience God for ourselves), still they are often suggestive. The stories and the teaching of the New Testament consistently imply that God intends for his grace to have a dynamic effect on our hearts, minds, and lives. God's love inspires love, his truth inspires confession, his goodness inspires morality, and so forth.

Consider just two biblical descriptions of the life-changing power of the grace of God in the life of believers. We've already looked at each of these passages earlier, but at this point, we can look at them again with one specific question in mind: what do they say about how believers' lives change when God's grace has touched them in a personal way?

> Praise be to the God and Father of our Lord Jesus Christ! In his great mercy he has given us new birth into a living hope through the resurrection of Jesus Christ from the dead, and into an inheritance that can never perish, spoil or fade—kept in heaven for you. . . . In this you greatly rejoice, though now for a little while you may have had to suffer grief in all kinds of trials. . . . Though you have not seen him, you love him; and even though you do not see him now, you believe in him and are filled with an inexpressible and glorious joy, for you are receiving the goal of your faith, the salvation of your souls.
>
> 1 Peter 1:3-6, 8-9 NIV

For the grace of God that brings salvation has appeared to all [people]. It teaches us to say "No" to ungodliness and worldly passions, and to live self-controlled, upright and godly lives in this present age, while we wait for the blessed hope—the glorious appearing of our great God and Savior, Jesus Christ, who gave himself for us to redeem us from all wickedness and to purify for himself a people that are his very own, eager to do what is good.

Titus 2:11-14 NIV

New birth, hope, joy, self-control, godly living, and eagerness to do good—all are the result of God's gracious activity in the life of a believer. We will always struggle with the temptation and impact of sin, but God enters into human lives in dynamic, life-changing ways, because God did not intend to save us from our sins and leave us in our sinful state as though nothing had happened. We need to come to believe that we are truly precious in God's eyes, dearly loved as his creation, and that we have a wonderful opportunity to grow and to serve through faith in Christ and the working of God in us and through us. Although no two people experience God's activity within them in exactly the same ways, those who have been awakened to God's presence and grace will be changed for the better, often beginning with a sense of love and forgiveness.

If you feel that your life is one big "have to" and you are tired of trying hard to prove your worth, or if you feel you are mired in sin or a sense of "quiet (or not so quiet) desperation," then you may be especially ready for God to surprise you with an experience of divine love and grace. We cannot control God's timing of when he will choose so to bless us, nor should we try to force ourselves to be ready to experience God. However, the more we are honest with our sense of dissatisfaction with our life, the more ready we become.

You may need to slow down enough to recognize your feelings of emptiness, shame, or desperation. You may need to stop trying to dull your senses or to cover up your pain with more work, more food or drink, more activity, or more of anything that would distract you from the pain of your soul. Whether by our choice or God's intervention, all of us need to come to the place where we truly want what only God can give. We need to learn to come to God with an open heart and mind, and with empty hands to receive whatever he has for us.

Sometimes I'll wake up in the night feeling horribly empty. I used to try to avoid the gnawing sense of void and longing with any thought whatsoever that would make me feel a little better—a happy memory, or perhaps a fantasy of some conquest or fulfilling experience. I might even gravitate to anxiety or second-guessing of myself at times, as troubling as such thoughts and feelings are, because they would distract me from the more painful feelings of emptiness and longing.

I've learned, though, that these moments are excellent opportunities for me, because they awaken me to my need for God. Now, when I have these experiences, I force myself to feel my feelings and try to stay with them as long as possible. Often they begin to subside as I face them and ask God to fill me in ways only God can. I may ask God to reveal the magnitude of his love and grace in some surprising way. As discussed in chapter 6, I may ask for eyes to see whatever I need to see (from God's perspective), courage to face the truth, and strength to act on what is revealed. Or I may simply repeat the name of Jesus.

Regardless of the prayer we choose in the moment, the dynamic is the same: we need to allow ourselves to face the emptiness, pain, and longing in our life without running from it, and then reach out to God to assure us of his love and acceptance. As the author of Hebrews urges, "Let us then approach the throne of grace with confidence, so that we may receive mercy and find grace to help us in our time of need" (Heb. 4:16 NIV).

What's Real

*The grace of God creates the only sure foundation for
personal transformation and dynamic spiritual leadership.*

Experiencing the gospel is the antidote to shame and the only sure foundation for our personal transformation and spiritual leadership. Paul could be ridiculed, rejected, and persecuted, but he walked with his head held high and drew people to him because of his experience with God's grace and his utter reliance on God's love and acceptance of him. He refused to take pride in himself to establish himself in his own eyes or the eyes of others. He rejected shame and despair even though he was well aware of his own sinfulness. Instead, he felt confidence and joy, because he took his identity and self-worth from God's gracious view of him, the only solid basis for a healthy self-image that stands up in light of God's perfect standards.

To Timothy, Paul wrote, "[O]f this gospel I was appointed a herald and an apostle and a teacher. That is why I am suffering as I am. Yet I am not ashamed, because I know whom I have believed, and am convinced that he is able to guard what I have entrusted to him for that day" (2 Tim. 1:11-12 NIV). To the Romans he declared, "I am not ashamed of the gospel, because it is the power of God for the salvation of everyone who believes: first for the Jew, then for the Gentile. For in the gospel a righteousness from God is revealed, a righteousness that is by faith from first to last, just as it is written: 'The righteous will live by faith'" (Rom. 1:16-17 NIV).

To the Philippians, Paul explained that even his great achievements, by the standards of the Pharisees, were meaningless to him in contrast to knowing Christ in an experiential way that was rooted in faith. That is, while he could find many things to boast about in the relative standards that people set up for one another, he cared only about his spiritual life, which came as a gift from God. His life was being transformed by his humbly accepting the righteousness that comes from faith in Christ and by his earnestly pursuing a relationship with Christ with all of his attention and energy:

> Whatever was to my profit I now consider loss for the sake of Christ. What is more, I consider everything a loss compared to the surpassing greatness of knowing Christ Jesus my Lord, for whose sake I have lost all things. I consider them rubbish, that I may gain Christ and be found in him, not having a righteousness of my own that comes from the

law, but that which is through faith in Christ—the righteousness that comes from God and is by faith. I want to know Christ and the power of his resurrection and the fellowship of sharing in his sufferings, becoming like him in his death, and so, somehow, to attain to the resurrection from the dead. Not that I have already obtained all this, or have already been made perfect, but I press on to take hold of that for which Christ Jesus took hold of me.

Philippians 3:8-12 NIV

Paul's hope rested entirely on the righteousness that God created in him through Christ and by his faith. Yet, his knowledge of Christ was not static or impersonal. He had a growing relationship, initiated by Christ and experienced in dynamic ways that were transforming him.

When we finally find our sense of well-being in God's gracious view of us (which is the good news of salvation by grace through faith), we do not need to be embarrassed or ashamed about our life or our spiritual leadership, regardless of what others may think about us. We will always have meaning and purpose. We will always have knowledge of God's love and a source of spiritual nurture. We will ultimately be secure, no matter what we may suffer along the way. We will be rooted in who God is and what God provides and not be dependent on our own efforts or on fluctuating feelings and moods.

Then, the more we experience the grace of God personally, the more we will be set free to love God from our hearts. Jesus explained this principle when he commented on the woman who anointed him with her tears: "Therefore, I tell you, her sins, which were many, have been forgiven; hence she has shown great love. But the one to whom little is forgiven, loves little" (Luke 7:47 NRSV). The more we are in touch with the magnitude of God's love and mercy, the more we will genuinely love God in return.

As we experience God's graciousness in a personal way, we will also become freer to accept others as they are and to show grace to them. If, on the other hand, we are still operating out of shame and feel that we have to perform well to feel good about ourselves, we will tend to expect other people around us—notably our spouse, children, and staff—to perform well, too. We may see them as extensions of ourselves and need them to act in a certain way so that we can feel good about ourselves. We may have no idea how much we are trying to control our spouse, our children, or our co-workers, but we are probably overcontrolling if we have unresolved shame in our lives and see them as reflections of ourselves. We simply won't escape feeling embarrassed by them if they don't "measure up" to whatever standards we have in our head or to those standards others try to impose on us.

If, instead, we rest in God's love and grace for our own sense of worth, we can let other people do the same. We will be set free from trying to make other people perform so that we can feel good about ourselves because of their performance. We will feel freer to accept them for who they are and to let them make their own choices about how they are going think and act. We may not agree with or appreciate what others do at times, but our own self-worth won't be linked to their choices; we will be freed to establish much healthier and more constructive relationships with them.

Our heartfelt love of God and our freedom from guilt and shame also greatly affect our ability to serve effectively as spiritual leaders of our ministries or organizations. While many skills are needed to lead well, our own experience with grace and our ability to express that grace to others are even more important to spiritual leadership. By experiencing as well as knowing the truth of the gospel, we can become effective catalysts for creating a vital spiritual environment in our workplace.

That is, the more we have experienced grace, mercy, and acceptance from God, the more we will be prepared to offer these same gifts to others and to promote an atmosphere of grace. The more we believe with heartfelt conviction that our worth is based on God's love and forgiveness, the more we will be ready to love and value our co-workers, constituents, and parishioners without judgment or condescension. As others experience grace from us, they will have more joy and will trust more in the goodness of God. As they see our example and experience graciousness from us, they will be more likely themselves to extend grace to others.

As leaders, we need to remember that gracious leadership does not lower standards for job performance or undermine the priority of getting results. Rather, grace means affirming a person's worth as a precious creation of God, dearly loved and redeemed through Christ, regardless of the level of his or her skills, intelligence, methods, looks, or personal mannerisms. Grace keeps us from shaming people or treating them as if they were worthless, deficient, or unimportant when we run into them at the water cooler, have to address job-performance issues, or relate to them in other contexts. Grace is about loving others as we ourselves have been loved.

Here's Help

Our best help to experience the grace of God ourselves and to become gracious spiritual leaders comes from God in the context of our relationship to God. In our own power, we cannot create an experience with God, because it can come only as a gift, in God's timing, regardless of our own sense of readiness or lack thereof. Sometimes we are completely surprised by God, and we are moved to tears or to joy without any sense of looking for or expecting God to touch our lives. At others times, we may have been pleading with God for years to speak to us or to help us in a certain way, but we experience only silence. We cannot control how and when God will choose to bless us with an experience of grace and love, or to bless those we affect through our leadership.

Nevertheless, the writer to the Hebrews suggests that when we act in faith by seeking God earnestly, we will experience more of God's blessings: "And without faith it is impossible to please God, because anyone who comes to him must believe that he exists and that he rewards those who earnestly seek him" (Heb. 11:6 NIV). Faith that pleases God and that God rewards, then, is an expectancy that drives us actively to seek God with our heart, mind, and actions.

In addition, we can cultivate a conscious relationship with the Holy Spirit, whom God has given to us to draw us to a greater knowledge, understanding, and experience of God. We can respond to the nudging, prodding, encouraging, convicting, convincing influence of the Holy Spirit in our life by accepting the divine messages we receive and acting on them. We recognize the Spirit's activity within us by its character, which Paul summarizes as the fruit of the Spirit: love, joy, peace, patience, kindness, goodness, faithfulness, gentleness, and self-control (Gal. 5:22-23 NIV). By the grace of God, we can say yes to God's prompting, and thus experience moments of transformed living, including such virtues as uprightness, godliness, and good deeds (Titus 2:11-14).

Paul sums up the dynamic nature of the Christian life simply as living by the Spirit. The more we experience the fruit of the Spirit and times of following the Spirit's leading, the more we will experience the abundant life we have longed for, which Paul describes at one point simply as "life and peace":

> Those who live according to the sinful nature have their minds set on what that nature desires; but those who live in accordance with the Spirit have their minds set on what the Spirit desires. The mind of sinful man is death, but the mind controlled by the Spirit is life and peace.
>
> Romans 8:5-6 NIV

Yet we must also remember that we experience God's greatest power and help when we are weakest, not strongest. As discussed in the previous chapter, I've had many disappointments, heartaches, and painful challenges in my life and leadership. At times, I've been chagrined at my inadequacy and my failures, and disappointed that I have not seen all the results I have hoped for. Nonetheless, my struggles have taught me to look to God in ways I probably never would have without them. I have come to experience God's love and grace in deeper ways and to see how much good can be done when I look to God to lead me in ways that I cannot plan. While my tendency is to value most highly whatever I can accomplish as a leader by my own intelligence, ingenuity, and hard work, my experience has taught me that what God does within me, my co-workers, and the beneficiaries of my leadership is far more important.

Our struggles, limitations, and painful experiences may be God's vehicles to bring us to the place of increasing dependence on God, where we can experience God's richest blessings and the greatest fruitfulness in our leadership. Paul eloquently expressed his positive experience of looking to God to work in and through him, amid his own limitations and the hardest moments in his ministry. God revealed to Paul that God works best when we have to rely on him. Paul wrote:

> But [the Lord] said to me, "My grace is sufficient for you, for my power is made perfect in weakness." Therefore I will boast all the more gladly about my weaknesses, so that Christ's power may rest on me. That is why, for Christ's sake, I delight in weaknesses, in insults, in hardships, in persecutions, in difficulties. For when I am weak, then I am strong.
>
> 2 Corinthians 12:9-10 NIV

Most of us have a long way to go to let go of our pride and selfishness, but God continually holds out hope to us, especially in our times of uncertainty, weakness, and even failure. That is what grace is all about—God's mercy and help in our time of need, and God's power at work through us irrespective of our own skills and capacity.

Paradoxically, to rely more on God does not diminish us, as we might fear. Far from it: when we are fully trusting in God to work through us, we feel freer than ever to use the gifts God has given us—work that results in fruitful ministry. The more we genuinely live to bring God glory, the more God's glory will shine through us, and the more we will let go of those things that diminish us—those foolish, vain, or misguided impulses to try to look good in others' eyes, to comfort ourselves in unhealthy ways, or to get caught up in other sins or distractions from our true calling. Thus, a life yielded to God's Spirit and dependent on God's grace for fruitful leadership and ministry results both in greater glory to God and in greater appreciation and honor for us.

In short, the best help we have to experience the love and grace of God and to become "grace-full" spiritual leaders is God. Our part is to seek God diligently, and God's part is nothing less than to give us the Holy Spirit. The more we learn to live by the Holy Spirit—cultivating a deeper spiritual life, practicing spiritual disciplines, aligning with God's purposes, seeking to create a vital spiritual environment in our workplace, obeying the Spirit's promptings when called to change, listening to God's voice in one another, trusting God always, and letting the grace of God transform us and the way we treat others—the more Spirit-filled our life and leadership will be.

Something to Think About

For leaders, our soul is the most precious part of who we are. It requires continual nurture and attention. Who we are, how we relate to God, what we think and feel about ourselves, how we set out to be in the world and conduct our life and leadership—all these grow out of our soul. The more vital our relationship to God, the healthier our soul, and the better able we are to be the spiritual leaders God intends for us to be.

Before you close this book, I encourage you to take a few more moments for reflection and prayer. You may want to begin by writing in your journal. Then, pray on your own or with your leadership team for God to continue the work that he has begun in your life and leadership.

In the quietness of this moment, open your heart and mind to God. Thank God for whatever he has shown you through your reading and reflection on the material in this book—insights that may help you deepen your own spiritual life. Thank God for his grace, mercy, and work in your life and leadership through the hard times as well as the easier times.

Ask for help to trust, to believe in your heart that God is your friend, has your best interests in mind, and is present and active in your life. Ask God for eyes to see what you need to see, for courage to face the truth, and for strength to act on what God reveals.

"May the grace of the Lord Jesus Christ, and the love of God, and the fellowship of the Holy Spirit be with you" as you seek to deepen spiritually and to grow in your ability to integrate your spiritual life and leadership and to be an effective Spirit-led leader.[2]

Appendix A

Lectio Divina: Divine Reading of Scripture

30–60 Minute Group Session

Six minutes: Silent prayer or preparation.

Eight minutes: During the first reading of a biblical text, group members listen for whatever word or concept jumps out at them. They then briefly share their "word" with each other, without commentary or discussion.

Eight minutes: During the second reading of the same text, listeners enter into the story with their imagination, as if they were present when the Scripture words were spoken or the events occurred. Again, after a time of silent reflection, the group members briefly share their experiences with one another.

Eight minutes: During the third reading, participants listen for what the Holy Spirit may be saying to them through the text about their present life. Group members have the option to offer their own spoken prayers after a few moments of silence.

20 minutes: Participants sit for 20 minutes of contemplation in total silence.

10 minutes: The session concludes with an open group discussion on the text and group members' experience, followed by a closing prayer.

The last two sections may be omitted to reduce the length of time for the *lectio divina* session.

Appendix B

The Spirit-Led Leader

Nine Leadership Practices with Corresponding Soul Principles

Leadership Practice 1

Envision your leadership flowing out of a deep spiritual life.

Soul Principle 1

Fruitfulness in leadership requires the work of God in and through us (Luke 2:46-49; 4:42-43; 5:15-16; 22:42; John 15:1-13; 1 Cor. 12:4-7; Phil. 2:12-13).

Leadership Practice 2

Actively cultivate your own spiritual life.

Soul Principle 2

Spiritual vitality flows from a real change of heart and mind toward God (Matt. 22:37-39; Col. 1:28-29; 3:17; Rom. 5:5; 8:13-14; 9:21; Phil. 2:5-11; Gal. 5:22-26; Heb. 5:7).

Leadership Practice 3

Develop specific spiritual disciplines.

Soul Principle 3

Disciplines deepen our spiritual life and empower
our leadership (2 Pet. 1:3-11).

Leadership Practice 4

Always seek to serve God's purposes first.

Soul Principle 4

Aligning our will with God's is an all-encompassing,
ongoing process (Col. 1:9-10; James 1:5-7).

Leadership Practice 5

Create a vital spiritual environment within your workplace.

Soul Principle 5

God works powerfully as we seek his activity among us (Acts
6:1-6; 13:1-3; 1 Cor. 12:1-7; 2 Cor. 12:9-10; Gal. 5:16-25;
Eph. 4:30–5:12; Phil. 2:1-8).

Leadership Practice 6

Make change a personal priority.

Soul Principle 6

Change is our calling (Mark 10:45; John 3:16; 5:24; Rom.
3:21-24; 5:1-6; 8:5-11; 12:1-2; Phil. 1:6; 2:12; Col. 1:9-12;
Titus 2:11-14).

Leadership Practice 7

Lead by listening well.

Soul Principle 7

The Holy Spirit speaks and works through every team member (1 Cor. 12; Phil. 2:3-8).

Leadership Practice 8

Always trust God.

Soul Principle 8

Steadfast trust in God is indispensable to spiritual vitality and leadership (Ps. 23; 42:5-6; 56:3-4; Prov. 3:5-6; Isa. 55:8-9; Jer. 17:28; Rom. 5:3-5; 8:28-39; 12:2; John 14:1; Heb. 6:13-15, 11:1; James 1:5-6; 1 Pet. 1:6-9).

Leadership Practice 9

Open yourself fully to the love and grace of God.

Soul Principle 9

The grace of God creates the only sure foundation for personal transformation and dynamic spiritual leadership (Eph. 2:8-9; 1 Pet. 1:3-6, 8-9; Titus 2:11-14; 2 Tim. 1:11-12; Heb. 4:16; 11:6; Rom. 1:16-17; 8:5-6; Phil. 3:8-12; 2 Cor. 12:9-10).

Notes

Introduction

1. Professionals burn out for a variety of reasons. Perhaps one of the most common is attempting to function for an extended period of time in spheres outside one's areas of giftedness. My point here is not to address the issue of burnout, but to give an example of the risks inherent in any culture or system that overfocuses on achievement and performance to the neglect of inner transformation and other important needs within the individual, organization, or team of co-workers.

2. My views of a healthy work environment have been influenced by a three-legged-stool model of resiliency for teenagers, which we have relied on in our work with youth at TreeHouse. One leg is a caring and supportive environment; the second is high but realistic expectations; and the third is opportunities to be involved—a way to contribute to society. See Bonnie Benard (who developed this model based on research with youth), *Fostering resiliency in kids: protective factors in the family, school and community* (Portland, Ore.: Northwest Regional Educational Laboratory [1991]); and Jean Antonello, *Getting Kids to Talk: Safe and Successful Teen Support Groups* (Plymouth, Minn.: Family Hope Services, 2004), 129–130.

3. According to the four Gospels, Jesus did not use any word that we would translate today as "spirituality." Nevertheless, he talked

about a quality of life and relationship to God that approximates the definition of spirituality that we are using here. Paul develops the concept of spirituality extensively in several of his epistles, drawing the connection between our relationship to God, the Holy Spirit, and the Christian spirituality of a spiritual person (*pneumatikos*). (See Rom. 1:11; 7:14; 15:27; 1 Cor. 2:13-14, 15; 3:1; 9:11; 10:3-4; 12:1; 14:1, 37; 15:44, 46; Gal. 6:1; Eph. 1:3; 5:19; 6:12; Col. 1:9; 3:16.) The only other New Testament authors to use a form of the term *pneumatikos* are Peter (1 Pet. 2:5) and the author of Revelation, a book in which the adverbial form seems to mean "figuratively" (Rev. 11:8).

4. See, for example, Mark 10:26-30. Jesus assures Peter that all those who sacrificed in this life would receive a hundred times as much in this age, and eternal life in the next age.

5. See appendix B for a complete list of the nine sets of leadership practices and soul principles addressed in each chapter.

Chapter 1

1. For example, see the description of fifth-level leaders (the highest level), who not only have strong professional competency and will, but who lead with self-effacing humility, in James C. Collins, *Good to Great: Why Some Companies Make the Leap . . . and Others Don't* (New York: HarperBusiness, 2001), 17–39.

2. Bill Thrall, Bruce McNichol, and Ken McElrath provide a compelling picture of the contrast between the "capacity" and "character" ladders of success, the need to prioritize the development of character, and the way to integrate the two ladders for maximum results in leadership (*The Ascent of a Leader: How Ordinary Relationships Develop Extraordinary Character and Influence* [San Francisco: Jossey-Bass, 1999], 31, 144). The authors emphasize the spiritual dimension of character throughout the book and especially stress the importance of trust in God and the creation of an environment of grace.

3. C. Michael Thompson, *The Congruent Life: Following the Inward Path to Fulfilling Work and Inspired Leadership* (San Francisco: Jossey-Bass, 2000), 10. By the "devoted inner life," Thompson means the spiritual life, which he describes at length. See especially chapter 10, "Personal Spiritual Growth," 234–266.

4. Specific methods to deepen our spiritual life are discussed at length in chapters 2 and 3. Spiritual practices and principles that can transform our leadership are the subject of chapters 4 through 9. At this point, creating a clear and compelling vision for ourselves as leaders and for our leadership is what's important.

5. James C. Collins describes the "Stockdale paradox" to make a similar point. Admiral Jim Stockdale, a prisoner of war at the "Hanoi Hilton" in Vietnam, survived by holding on to a vision of eventually prevailing over his captors and escaping, even while he faced the brutal facts of everyday life in captivity (*Good to Great*, 83–87).

6. See Robert S. McGee's insightful work *The Complete Search for Significance: Seeing Your True Worth through God's Eyes* (Houston: Rapha Publishing, 1994). McGee explores the human fear of failure and fear of rejection that lead to a preoccupation with performance and efforts to please others. At the core of these fears and misplaced goals is shame, the remedy for which is a true understanding and experience of God's unconditional love and Christ's saving work of redemption. See chapter 9 for a fuller discussion of shame and grace and how they affect self-image, relationships, and leadership.

7. Spiritual leaders will be more effective in fostering spiritual transformation in others if they are aware of the various dimensions of spirituality, including styles and preferences, among the people with whom they are working. Corinne Ware discusses helpful transformational goals that correspond to four key spirituality preferences found among the population at large in her book for spiritual directors and congregational leaders, *Discover Your Spiritual Type* (Bethesda: Alban Institute, 1995), 37–45. To oversimplify the categories, we may say that some people prefer learning (knowledge); some, feeling; others, contemplating; and still others, activism or serving. While individuals gravitate to one or more of these ways of knowing and worshiping God, Christians, including leaders, can deepen and enrich their relationship with God by cultivating all four dimensions. See, too, John Ackerman's helpful suggestions for fostering spiritual transformation in congregations, which draw on Ware's four categories of spiritual types, in *Listening to God: Spiritual Formation in Congregations* (Bethesda: Alban Institute, 2001), 43–57.

8. Examples of Peter's Spirit-led and Spirit-empowered leadership include stories told in Acts 4:8-12; 5:1-7; 8:17; 9:34; 9:40; 10; 15:7-12. Stories of Paul's experiences are told in Acts 13–28 and in his epistles, where he makes frequent mention of the work of the Holy Spirit in his life and leadership.

9. See Luke 2:46-49; 4:42-43; 5:15-16; 22:42; Philippians 2:5-11; Hebrews 12:2.

Chapter 2

1. Dallas Willard, *The Spirit of the Disciplines: Understanding How God Changes Lives* (San Francisco: HarperSanFrancisco, 1988), 14.

2. Martin L. Smith, *The Word Is Very Near You: A Guide to Praying with Scripture* (Cambridge, Mass.: Cowley Publications, 1989), 19–22.

3. Ibid, 18.

4. Ibid.

5. Ibid., 21-22.

6. Ibid., 19.

7. See, for example, Romans 8:38-39 and Ephesians 1:3–14.

8. See the "Here's Help" section in this chapter, and also see chapter 9 on how we can come to love God better by more fully experiencing God's love for us. See chapter 8 on how we can choose to trust God, even amid suffering and uncertainty in our life.

9. For the explicit call to submit to God, see James 4:7. In Romans 10:3, Paul implies that responding affirmatively to the gospel is equated with submitting to God's righteousness. Paul thinks it important even to stress that Christ, as Son of God, will ultimately be made subject to God the Father at the end of time, so that "God may be all in all" (1 Cor. 15:28). In addition, well over 100 verses in the Bible, from Genesis to Revelation, speak of the necessity of obeying God.

10. C. Michael Thompson, *The Congruent Life: Following the Inward Path to Fulfilling Work and Inspired Leadership* (San Francisco: Jossey-Bass, 2000), 58.

11. Brother Lawrence, *The Practice of the Presence of God: Conversations and Letters of Brother Lawrence* (Oxford, England: Oneworld Publications, 1999), 2–3, 74. Original edition published in 1692.

12. Ibid., 12.

13. Ibid., 10, 32.

14. Ibid., 20.

15. Ibid., 9.

16. M. Craig Barnes, *Searching for Home: Spirituality for Restless Souls* (Grand Rapids: Brazos Press, 2003), 33. Barnes puts it this way: "Home is the place where we were created to live from eternity and for eternity—with our true Family of Father, Son and Holy Spirit."

17. Brother Lawrence, *The Practice of the Presence of God*, 24–26, 63, 79.

18. Ibid., 30, 46.

19. Ibid., 31.

20. Ibid., 33.

21. Ibid., 47, 81.

22. Ibid., 47, 78–79.

23. Ibid., 47.

24. Ibid., 56, 58.

25. Ibid., 72–75.

26. Ibid., 90, 112.

27. Ibid., 101–105.

28. Gerald G. May, *The Awakened Heart: Opening Yourself to the Love You Need* (San Francisco: HarperSanFrancisco, 1991); see especially 133-211.

29. May, *The Awakened Heart*, 133–134.

30. Brother Lawrence, *The Practice of the Presence of God*, 33.

31. May, *The Awakened Heart*, 157.

32. Brother Lawrence, *The Practice of the Presence of God*, 56, 58.

33. May, *The Awakened Heart*, 158–159. May notes that biblical antecedents to this prayer may include Psalm 22:19; Mark 10:47; and Luke 18:13. For a fuller discussion of the roots and theology of the Jesus prayer, see Tony Jones, *The Sacred Way* (Grand Rapids: Zondervan, 2005), 59–66.

34. Brother Lawrence, *The Practice of the Presence of God*, 72–75.

35. May, *The Awakened Heart*, 167.

36. Brother Lawrence, *The Practice of the Presence of God*, 41–42.

37. Ibid., 90, 112.

38. May, *The Awakened Heart*, 211.

39. Smith, *The Word Is Very Near You*, 37.

40. Ibid., 47.

41. Ibid., 51.

42. Ibid., 51–52.

43. For numerous practical suggestions on how to go about contemplative prayer, see Smith, *The Word Is Very Near You*, 130–142; and May, *The Awakened Heart*, 196–206.

44. Brother Lawrence, *The Practice of the Presence of God*, 47.

45. For additional suggestions, including group exercises, on practicing the presence of God in many contexts of life and work, see Tilden Edwards, *Living in the Presence: Spiritual Exercises to Open Our Lives to the Awareness of God* (San Francisco: HarperSanFrancisco, 1995).

Chapter 3

1. Richard J. Foster, *Celebration of Discipline: The Path to Spiritual Growth* (New York: Harper & Row, 1978).

2. Dallas Willard, *The Spirit of the Disciplines: Understanding How God Changes Lives* (San Francisco: HarperSanFrancisco, 1988), 68. Willard addresses the subject of spiritual disciplines by drawing on theological, philosophical, and psychological perspectives. He stresses the necessity for Christians actively to cultivate their spiritual life to experience the abundant and fruitful life Christ intended for his followers.

3. See especially the writings of the apostle Paul, who talks about the presence of the Holy Spirit in the lives of believers (Eph. 1:13). If Christ dwells in us, the Holy Spirit gives us power over sin and produces a new quality of life that is better aligned with God's character and values (Rom. 6:5-6; 8:6-16; Gal. 5:16-25). Our salvation is the result of the grace of God, and our life of good works comes from God's working in us through Jesus Christ to make us capable of fulfilling his good will for our life (Eph. 2:8-10).

4. The typical pattern in Paul's letters is to begin with doctrinal material and to conclude with practical exhortations. Examples of his instructions on living out the Christian life can be found in Romans 6; 12–15; Galations 5–6; Ephesians 4–6; Philippians 1:27–2:18; 3:1–4:9; Colossians 2:6–4:6; 1 Thessalonians 4–5; and interspersed with doctrinal teaching throughout 1–2 Corinthians. Other New

Testament writers clearly call believers to draw close to God (e.g., Heb. 10:22; James 4:8) and to develop attitudes and actions that are consistent with Christian faith. Examples include Hebrews 10:19-39; 12–13; throughout James; 1 Peter 1:13–5:13; 1 John 2:18–4:21; Revelation 2–3.

5. It is precisely for this need to be freed from the power of sin in our life that spiritual disciplines were created. As Richard J. Foster puts it, disciplines are a door to liberation from ingrained habits and debased thinking, to "move beyond surface living into the depths" (*Celebration of Discipline*, 1).

6. Paul's letters are full of exhortations to make an effort to draw on God's power to seek transformation and to become more godly. As mentioned earlier, Paul exhorts the Ephesians to put off the old self and put on the new self, created by God to be like God (4:22-24). Paul charges the Romans, in view of God's mercy, "to offer your bodies as living sacrifices . . . [and] be transformed by the renewing of your mind" (Rom. 12:1-2, NIV). He warns the Corinthians to be careful not "to fall" (into sin), but to take the way God provides to escape the temptation (1 Cor. 10:12-13). After clarifying that their hope of salvation and possession of the Holy Spirit came from faith and not their human effort, and that they were "children of God through faith in Christ Jesus" (Gal. 3:1-3; 4:26), he goes on to urge the Galatians to "live by the Spirit" (5:16) and "keep in step with the Spirit" (5:25 NIV). His instructions include an imperative and hortatory subjunctive, respectively; the two verb forms suggest that human action is needed and expected.

7. Willard, *The Spirit of the Disciplines*, 20.

8. Foster, *Celebration of Discipline*, 6–7.

9. Foster, *Celebration of Discipline.* See, too, Henri J. M. Nouwen, *The Way of the Heart: Desert Spirituality and Contemporary Ministry* (New York: Seabury Press, 1981); and Willard, *The Spirit of the Disciplines.*

10. For one helpful contemporary guide, see Tony Jones, *The Sacred Way: Spiritual Practices for Everyday Life* (Grand Rapids: Zondervan, 2005). My wife, Jill Kimberly Hartwell Geoffrion, has written extensively on using the labyrinth as a spiritual tool. See especially her *Christian Prayer and Labyrinths: Pathways to Faith, Hope and Love* (Cleveland: Pilgrim Press, 2004).

11. You can also practice *lectio divina* by yourself and in smaller time chunks, by allowing less time between the readings, by abbreviating or eliminating the 20-minute meditation section, or even by omitting the debriefing segment at the end. For other ways to think about and practice *lectio divina*, see Tony Jones, *The Sacred Way*, 47–55.

Chapter 4

1. Rick Warren, *The Purpose-Driven Life* (Grand Rapids: Zondervan, 2002), 17.

2. Rudolf Bultmann, *Theology of the New Testament* (New York: Scribners, 1951–1955), 9, 12, 285.

3. Bill Hybels, Conference on Preaching and Teaching, Willow Creek Community Church, South Barrington, Ill., Oct. 18, 2004.

4. Larry Crabb, *Connecting: A Radical New Vision* (Nashville: W Publishing Group, 1997), 103–126. In these pages Crabb discusses "four urges to be killed" that he describes through metaphor—city building: the urge to prove one's adequacy; fire lighting: the urge to establish our reputation by building others' confidence in us; wall whitewashing: the urge to secure one's safety; and well digging: the urge to pursue our own pleasure and satisfaction.

5. By extension of Old and New Testament examples, we may expect God to call and enable believers to fulfill God's purposes in the world, in and outside the church.

In the Hebrew Scriptures (Old Testament), God raised up leaders by empowering them with his Spirit or by making their leadership successful by divine intervention in one way or another. Moses, Joshua, Gideon, Samson, Deborah, David, and Solomon are well-known examples.

In the New Testament, we read that Jesus called his disciples and sent them out (hence their designation as "apostles," which means "sent out ones") with power to conduct fruitful ministry (see Luke 9:1). Similarly God called individuals to mission work through prophets in the early church (see Acts 13:2) or through dreams and visions (see Acts 16:10). When the Holy Spirit began to dwell within believers after Pentecost, Paul emphasized spiritual gifts for ministry (1 Cor. 12; Rom. 12:3-8; Eph. 4:6-16). Most of these gifts were for strengthening the believers in their faith and knowledge of the faith, though at least one, evangelism, was designed for nonbelievers. Paul also referred to God's calling or appointing of individuals to various roles and positions, including administration, outside the church, and explicit Christian ministry (see 1 Cor. 7:17-24; Rom. 13:1-2).

6. Gary Friesen, in *Decision Making and the Will of God: A Biblical Alternative to the Traditional View* (Portland, Ore.: Multnomah, 1980).

7. For an excellent resource to help pastors and church leaders to seek God actively in the course of discernment, decision-making, and conducting other congregational business, see John Ackerman, *Listening to God: Spiritual Formation in Congregations* (Bethesda: Alban Institute, 2001).

8. Larry Crabb, *Connecting*, 108.

9. James C. Collins, *Good to Great: Why Some Companies Make the Leap . . . and Others Don't* (New York: HarperCollins, 2001), 65.

Chapter 5

1. James C. Collins, *Good to Great: Why Some Companies Make the Leap. . . and Others Don't* (New York: HarperCollins, 2001), 41.

2. I am indebted to my spiritual director, John Ackerman, for this practice of encouraging committee members to anticipate that God will be at work in the course of an administrative meeting and then to reflect on their experience afterward. Ackerman offers many insights on seeking corporate discernment and on nurturing a spiritually sensitive corporate environment in his book *Listening to God: Spiritual Formation in Congregations* (Herndon, Va.: Alban Institute, 2001).

3. A few suggestions for excellent books to read that promote personal and spiritual growth without being sectarian include Stephen R. Covey, *The Seven Habits of Highly Effective People: Powerful Lessons in Personal Change* (New York: Free Press, 2004); Joseph Jaworski, *Synchronicity: The Inner Path of Leadership* (San Francisco: Berrett Koehler Publishing, 1996); Robert E. Quinn, *Deep Change: Discovering the Leader Within* (San Francisco: Jossey-Bass, 1996); Peter M. Senge, *The Fifth Discipline: The Art and Practice of the Learning Organization* (New York: Doubleday/Currency, 1990);

and C. Michael Thompson, *The Congruent Life: Following the Inward Path to Fulfilling Work and Inspired Leadership* (San Francisco: Jossey-Bass, 2000).

4. In the New Testament, "flesh" (*sarks*) can refer simply to the human body (e.g., Matt. 19:5-6), to the natural source of human strength and abilities (e.g., Matt. 16:7), or to sinful impulses within a person (Rom. 8:5-8). "Flesh" can be neutral or even positive as a simple description of material being, as opposed to spiritual being (e.g., John 1:14; Acts 2:17). However, the apostle Paul speaks of human "flesh" largely in derogatory terms, as an independent power within a person that leads to actions contrary to the will of God and opposed to the leading of the Holy Spirit (e.g., Gal. 5:16-21).

Chapter 6

1. In contrast, the "Emerging Church" phenomenon is attempting to reach adults through new ways of thinking, communicating, and creative experimentation. For example, see Mike Breen and Walt Kallestad, *The Passionate Church: The Art of Life-Changing Discipleship* (Colorado Springs: NexGen of Cook Communication Ministries, 2005). Breen and Kallestad offer LifeShapes as a creative visual tool for discipleship, and argue that millions of people in their 20s and 30s will not attend a typical church because they experience church as shallow and unable to meet their needs for community. Another leader in the Emerging Church movement, author and pastor Brian McLaren, offers new ways for the church to be both committed to Jesus Christ and more culturally relevant and effective in reaching nonbelievers. Regardless of whether we agree with everything that writers within the Emerging Church have proposed, they rightly call the church to think in fresh ways. You can check out McLaren's Web site for many recommendations for resources at www.anewkindofchristian.com.

2. Robert E. Quinn, *Deep Change: Discovering the Leader Within* (San Francisco, Jossey-Bass, 1996).

3. Ibid., 78.

4. Ibid., 176.

5. Ibid., 177.

6. Ibid., 7.

7. James C. Collins and Jerry I. Porras, *Built to Last: Successful Habits of Visionary Companies* (New York: HarperCollins, 1994, 1997), popularized the notion of a BHAG, which originally stood for "Big Hairy Audacious Goal," which our staff borrowed and renamed "Big Holy Audacious Goal." Companies that outperformed their competitors significantly over the past century all had BHAGs that significantly exceeded the current capacity of the organization and the imagination of many within it.

8. See chapter 4, pages 86–88, "Always seek to serve God's purposes first."

9. The concept of servant leadership is of course well known today. See Robert K. Greenleaf, *The Servant as Leader* (Indianapolis: Robert K. Greenleaf Center, 1991), which is based on his groundbreaking 1970 essay of the same title.

10. Bennett J. Sims, *Servanthood: Leadership for a Third Millennium* (Boston: Cowley Publications, 1997), 37.

11. Quinn, *Deep Change*, 204.

Chapter 7

1. See Robert E. Quinn's thoughts on the inner voice of an organization, which honestly expresses what will lead to the success of the company as opposed to the inner voice of the leader, which sometimes is egocentric and driven by self-interest. Quinn also gives a helpful illustration of how leaders can draw on the voice of the organization to lead more effectively (*Deep Change: Discovering the Leader Within* [San Francisco: Jossey-Bass, 1996], 200–213).

2. James C. Collins addresses the importance of creating a corporate culture in which truth can be expressed and heard. The four basic practices he observed in successful companies are to lead with questions, not answers; to engage in dialogue and debate, not coercion; to conduct autopsies, without blame; and to build "red flag" mechanisms that allow staff to speak up when necessary to bring out information that cannot be ignored (*Good to Great: Why Some Companies Make the Leap. . . and Others Don't* [New York: HarperCollins, 2001], 73–80).

3. Peter M. Senge, *The Fifth Discipline: The Art and Practice of the Learning Organization* (New York: Doubleday/Currency, 1990).

Senge is on the cutting edge of thinking about transforming the workplace by making it a learning organization on every level. He is a champion of viewing organizations holistically, which leads to valuing the continual growth and contribution of every team member in setting direction, as opposed to the traditional model of leadership by one or a few.

4. Stephen R. Covey, *The Seven Habits of Highly Effective People: Powerful Lessons in Personal Change* (New York: Free Press, 2004).

5. See Romans 12:3-7; 1 Corinthians 12.

6. Patrick M. Lencioni, *Overcoming the Five Dysfunctions of a Team: A Field Guide for Leaders, Managers, and Facilitators* (San Francisco: Jossey-Bass, 2005), 7.

7. See the discussion beginning on page 152 on the importance of being genuinely open to others when we listen.

8. See the discussion of reflective listening on page 157.

9. See Eugene Raudsepp's article "Hone Listening Skills to Boost Your Career" at The Wall Street Journal Executive Career Site (www.careerjournal.com/myc/climbing/20021224-raudsepp) for some good tips on improving listening skills. For a self-assessment, try the Listening Skills Quiz: www.careerjournal.com/sidebars/20021224-raudsepp-quiz. (Web sites accessed July 2005).

10. See the discussion beginning on page 164 on the constructive role of conflict in discussions.

11. See the many suggestions in chapter 5 for seeking God together as a work team by creating a vital spiritual environment in the workplace, which includes prayer.

Chapter 9

1. Jeff VanVonderen served as a chemical dependency counselor at Family Hope Services' Passages clinic in the 1980s. His books include *Good News for the Chemically Dependent and for Those Who Love Them* (Minneapolis: Bethany House, 2004) and *Tired of Trying to Measure Up: Getting Free from the Demands, Expectations, and Intimidations of Well-Meaning People* (Minneapolis: Bethany House, 1989). In the 1990s, he conducted seminars on "Breaking the Silence" to help people overcome shame and painful childhood experiences.

2. Based on 2 Corinthians 13:14.

Selected Bibliography

Ackerman, John. *Listening to God: Spiritual Formation in Congregations.* Bethesda: Alban Institute, 2001. This book is particularly helpful for pastors and other spiritual leaders who want to help congregations learn how to listen to God in the context of community. Ackerman offers helpful insights into various preferences of worship styles to increase the leader's ability to work with all members of the congregation.

Anderson, Leith. *Leadership That Works: Hope and Direction for Church and Parachurch Leaders in Today's Complex World.* Minneapolis: Bethany House, 1999. Leith offers wisdom and insight on practical leadership from decades of experience as a highly effective leader of a large, suburban church. The book won *Christianity Today's* "Church/Pastoral Leadership Book of the Year" award in 2000.

Antonello, Jean. *Getting Kids to Talk: Safe and Successful Teen Support Groups.* Plymouth, Minn.: Family Hope Services, 2004. Antonello interviewed Family Hope Services' TreeHouse youth outreach staff to identify the chief principles and practices that create an environment in which youth will feel safe enough to talk about their pain and struggles. At the core of successful teen support groups is a nonjudgmental attitude and an atmosphere of grace.

Blackaby, Henry T., and Claude V. King. *Experiencing God: How to Live the Full Adventure of Knowing and Doing the Will of God.* Nashville: Broadman & Holman, 1994. Blackaby draws on years of pastoral experience in his best-selling resource for individuals and congregations. He gives practical guidelines for an experiential relationship with God. He urges readers to look for places where God is actively working and to join God there.

Collins, James C. *Good to Great: Why Some Companies Make the Leap . . . and Others Don't.* New York: HarperBusiness, 2001. Collins and his team of researchers provide significant insights into what makes a good company become a great company. His extensive research covers many leading American companies of the 20th century. I highly recommend this best-selling and highly respected book for leaders and organizations in the nonprofit world as well as in business.

Covey, Stephen R. *The Seven Habits of Highly Effective People: Powerful Lessons in Personal Change.* New York: Free Press, 2004. This updated version of Covey's well-known classic work is a helpful resource in accomplishing goals and working effectively with other people. The wisdom of his insights is immediately apparent in this readable and practical tool.

Crabb, Larry. *Connecting: A Radical New Vision.* Nashville: W Publishing Group, 1997. Crabb writes out of years of experience as a psychotherapist. He argues that there would be less need for psychotherapy if ordinary Christians learned how better to "connect" with one another in meaningful relationships of mutual care.

de Caussade, Jean-Pierre. *The Sacrament of the Present Moment.* Translated by Kitty Muggeridge from the original text of *Self-Abandonment to Divine Providence* (1966). San Francisco: Harper & Row, 1981. This short book comes from material taken from the talks and letters of Father Jean-Pierre de Caussade in 18th-century France. Caussade offers many practical insights into the mystical life for the person who desires to live in a sense of continual communion with God. His writings powerfully call believers both to submit to the divine will and to act—responding with love and obedience as God reveals his will moment by moment.

Dreyer, Elizabeth A., and Mark S. Burrows, eds. *Minding the Spirit: The Study of Christian Spirituality*. Baltimore: Johns Hopkins University Press, 2005. Professors Dreyer and Burrows have drawn together 25 contemporary essays exploring Christian spirituality, written by top scholars. *Minding the Spirit* demonstrates that spirituality is a serious academic subject for students and teachers, as well as for leaders and others in the practical field.

Foster, Richard J. *Celebration of Discipline: The Path to Spiritual Growth*. New York: Harper & Row, 1978. This book is the modern classic on spiritual disciplines. Foster provides an excellent orientation to these practices for the newcomer to faith as well as for those who are eager to grow spiritually.

Geoffrion, Jill Kimberly Hartwell. *Christian Prayer and Labyrinths: Pathways to Faith, Hope and Love*. Cleveland: Pilgrim Press, 2004. This is just one of seven published books by this author that offer many practical tools for appreciating and using the labyrinth as a spiritual resource. This volume provides an explicitly Christian perspective on walking the labyrinth and maximizing the opportunities it affords those who seek God on its path.

Jones, Tony. *The Sacred Way: Spiritual Practices for Everyday Life*. Grand Rapids: Zondervan, 2005. *The Sacred Way* provides an excellent introduction to spiritual practices in contemporary language. In a down-to-earth style, Jones shares his own journey and offers many practical suggestions, along with thoughtful commentary on ancient practices that are still relevant to the person who feels drawn by God to develop a deeper spiritual life.

Lawrence, Brother. *The Practice of the Presence of God*. Various publishers of hardcover and paperback editions. This little book is a classic guide to living with a continual sense of awareness of God throughout one's day in all circumstances. Lawrence learned how to adore God and to notice God's activity in his life amid the mundane. The book offers many of his insights and practices.

Lencioni, Patrick M. *Overcoming the Five Dysfunctions of a Team: A Field Guide for Leaders, Managers, and Facilitators*. San Francisco: Jossey-Bass, 2005. In this book Lencioni follows up his best-selling narrative, *The Five Dysfunctions of a Team*, with many practical suggestions. He zeroes in on key issues that inhibit teams from working productively together and offers down-to-earth insights and stepping stones to make teamwork more fruitful and to transform team relationships.

May, Gerald G. *Addiction and Grace: Love and Spirituality in the Healing of Addictions.* New York: HarperCollins, 1988. A former psychiatrist and spiritual guide, May provides piercing insight into the physiological and emotional quality of addictions of all kinds, from the well-known addictions to alcohol to what some might consider minor compulsions, such as addictions to watching movies or eating desserts. Hope for addicts—which include everyone, in his opinion—comes from God's grace to help us release us from the hold addictions have on us.

———. *The Awakened Heart: Opening Yourself to the Love You Need.* San Francisco: HarperSanFrancisco, 1991. In *The Awakened Heart*, May guides readers to look to God to meet our needs for love. This book offers an extended discussion of Brother Lawrence's practices.

McGee, Robert S. *The Complete Search for Significance: Seeing Your True Worth through God's Eyes.* Houston: Rapha Publishing, 1994. McGee offers penetrating insight into human fears, shame, and our need to feel significant. His book is both a theoretical and a practical tool to help readers overcome their fears and to trust in God's love, redemption, and sanctification to be secure and to feel significant.

Myra, Harold, and Marshall Shelley. *The Leadership Secrets of Billy Graham.* Grand Rapids: Zondervan, 2005. This engaging and challenging book offers solid leadership principles against the backdrop of the life and ministry of one of the most influential Christian leaders of the past century. The accompanying study guide provides many helpful ways to reflect on the insights found in the book.

Quinn, Robert E. *Deep Change: Discovering the Leader Within.* San Francisco: Jossey-Bass, 1996. Quinn draws on business experience to illustrate the serious danger of not changing, which leads to "slow death." His argument is compelling, and his illustrations are helpful to those who want to come to grips with the need for change within themselves and in their organizations.

Sanders, J. Oswald. *Spiritual Leadership: Principles of Excellence for Every Believer*, second revision. Chicago: Moody Press, 1994. This work is an updated version of an earlier collection of talks Sanders gave to the Overseas Missionary Fellowship staff in the 1960s. In it he describes many traits of a leader who is a genuinely spiritual person. He draws heavily on biblical references and principally British political and military leaders for insights and illustrations. The book is immensely readable and contains well-grounded guidance for any Christian leader.

Senge, Peter M. *The Fifth Discipline: The Art and Practice of the Learning Organization.* New York: Doubleday/Currency 1990. Management guru Peter Senge, in his seminal work on the "learning organization," stresses that companies excel and leadership teams thrive when executives learn to communicate, collaborate, and be humble enough to learn from others' experience and thinking.

Smith, Martin L. *The Word Is Very Near You: A Guide to Praying with Scripture.* Cambridge, Mass.: Cowley Publications, 1989. An Episcopal priest and author, Smith helps readers to understand that God takes the initiative in communicating with us. We can respond out of a sense of continuing the conversation God began. Smith offers practical tools and suggestions for praying with Scripture.

Thompson, C. Michael. *The Congruent Life: Following the Inward Path to Fulfilling Work and Inspired Leadership.* San Francisco: Jossey-Bass, 2000. Thompson runs a private consulting practice that focuses on organizational and individual leadership development; he also works with the Center for Creative Leadership. *The Congruent Life* is filled with helpful insights and illustrations on personal fulfillment and successful leadership based on an integrated life, characterized at the core by a vibrant spirituality.

Thrall, Bill, Bruce McNichol, and Ken McElrath. *The Ascent of a Leader: How Ordinary Relationships Develop Extraordinary Character and Influence.* San Francisco: Jossey-Bass, 1999. *The Ascent of a Leader* contrasts the ladder of capacity to the ladder of character. While most leaders start out trying to increase their capacity to advance in status and responsibilities, the authors argue that developing one's character is even more important.

Ultimately, the successful leader will integrate capacity and character.

VanVonderen, Jeff. *Good News for the Chemically Dependent and for Those Who Love Them*. Minneapolis: Bethany House, 2004. This book truly is good news for anyone who suffers from a chemical dependency. VanVonderen provides answers to the many questions facing those with addictions and those looking to help them—answers that grow out of years of experience counseling and conducting interventions.

————. *Tired of Trying to Measure Up: Getting Free from the Demands, Expectations, and Intimidations of Well-Meaning People*. Minneapolis: Bethany House, 1989. VanVonderen emphasizes the power of finding healing and wholeness by the grace of God. By contrast, if we allow ourselves and our relationships to be controlled by shame and the expectations of others, we will flounder powerlessly.

Willard, Dallas. *The Spirit of the Disciplines: Understanding How God Changes Lives*. San Francisco: HarperSanFrancisco, 1988. A professor of philosophy at the University of Southern California and a nationally known speaker on spiritual growth, Willard presents a powerful and challenging book calling Christians to take responsibility for their own spiritual maturity. Action is required for those who want to develop character and to live fruitful lives.